*H*THE PATH OF *appiness*

For Single Parents and Their Families

Trudy Joy

BALBOA.
PRESS
A DIVISION OF HAY HOUSE

This book is a work of non-fiction. Unless otherwise noted, the author and the publisher make no explicit guarantees as to the accuracy of the information contained in this book and in some cases, names of people and places have been altered to protect their privacy.

Balboa Press books may be ordered through booksellers or by contacting:

Balboa Press
A Division of Hay House
1663 Liberty Drive
Bloomington, IN 47403
www.balboapress.com
1 (877) 407-4847

Because of the dynamic nature of the Internet, any web addresses or links contained in this book may have changed since publication and may no longer be valid. The views expressed in this work are solely those of the author and do not necessarily reflect the views of the publisher, and the publisher hereby disclaims any responsibility for them.

The author of this book does not dispense medical advice or prescribe the use of any technique as a form of treatment for physical, emotional, or medical problems without the advice of a physician, either directly or indirectly. The intent of the author is only to offer information of a general nature to help you in your quest for emotional and spiritual well-being. In the event you use any of the information in this book for yourself, which is your constitutional right, the author and the publisher assume no responsibility for your actions.

Any people depicted in stock imagery provided by Thinkstock are models, and such images are being used for illustrative purposes only.
Certain stock imagery © Thinkstock.

Print information available on the last page.

ISBN: 978-1-5043-8625-8 (sc)
ISBN: 978-1-5043-8661-6 (e)

Library of Congress Control Number: 2017912922

Balboa Press rev. date: 08/28/2017

NURTURE FOR SINGLE PARENTS

Part 1

This book is lovingly dedicated to my soul's Angel, my daughter

With special thanks to my beautiful family
and friends for all their support

It has been lovingly written for all those
experiencing the single parent journey

Contents

FOREWORD

Introducing Me

I ntroductions are funny things, as one doesn't really know how much to bare of oneself in an initial meeting.

It may be seen by those who know the correct etiquette as a little classless – and probably a little overly-familiar to offload your life tales onto someone within the first five minutes of a meeting. That it would not be the correct protocol. Thankfully I am probably not always polite or correct in my etiquette, so I am going to launch straight in with baring my soul to you.

When I was young I rode horses, I jumped horses and I fell off horses a lot. And every time I fell of those crazy beasts, I would get back on and try and get its' stubborn arse over the jumps. I fell and then I got back on. Hurt bruised and embarrassed, I kept getting back on, hoping that this time I would sail over the four-foot fence effortlessly. On occasions my will won and on others the horse's defiance got the better to me and I would find myself in A&E. Little did I know that those actions would set the theme for my life. I would get knocked down and I would get up and try again and as I got older, I would bury the hurt and the humiliation. As a child in the 1980s with dyslexia, I was ridiculed by my teachers and peers for being stupid. By 15 I had been written off as a failure to the Great British education system. By 15 I had an overwhelming sense of personal failure, both for my parents and myself. At 17 I was living in London working as a chef hidden away in the heat of the kitchen. Cooking was something that I could excel in. I felt comfortable. Restaurant kitchens were the perfect hiding place for other misfits just like me. I was lifted by some and beaten down by those male chefs who were haunted by the ideals of chauvinism, who didn't believe that kitchens were places for girls. By 21 I was leading teams of chefs in London restaurants.

Fast forward to my mid-twenties and I had a spiritual epiphany, a spiritual awakening, which took me on a journey of self-discovery to India. This was a trip that would change my life. I met with the holy men and divine mothers, and experienced love that I had never felt before. I was overwhelmed by the grace, the miracles, and for the first time I felt a sense of peace with myself. The broken parts of me seemed to heal in the presence of this Divine love. It was on this first trip to India that I met my future husband, the man who would give me the biggest gift of my life and then destroy me in the process. Not only did I meet my future ex-husband on that trip, I also found a comfort and a knowing of a spiritual reality, a reality of unseen helpers that always seems to show up in my life when I need them to. To this day, I am sure that I am alive due to some unseen intervention in my darkest times.

From the moment I saw my husband I was in love. There seemed something so deep and profound between our two hearts that it was beyond the level of personality. The attraction went beyond the rational. He was the most beautiful man I had ever seen, my heart erupted with love for this perfect specimen of a man that triggered my feelings of self-worth, and personal shame at my own shortcomings. Miraculously when those feelings became suppressed, I could summon the courage to answer his questions without stammering over my words and I could meet him in the heart and allow myself to fall in love with him. I am not sure what motivated my husband to love me back at the time. I thought that we were soulmates, that he was the one, and I thought that if I felt it, he must have felt it too. And probably he did. For years we travelled backwards and forwards between the two continents, and survived by embracing our differences – and there were many – yet love seemed to unite our opposites for a time. After we married, we set up home in the UK, which was a huge change for him and in my naivety, I didn't release that I couldn't ever tame a man with a nomadic nature. Within the marriage arena, fear of his own abilities to be a responsible father and husband overtook the man I had fallen in love with. I was living with a stranger. He made bad, reckless and misguided choices. He allowed his anger to take over his rational mind. I supported him through all his stupid financial decisions. I allowed him to control, dominate and abuse me. In loving him, I lost myself. I found every excuse to stay with him, but mainly it was for my daughter, who loved her daddy. When it all got too much and I could no longer live with the fear for being used as a human pin cushion, I mustered up enough courage to pack him a bag, buy him a plane ticket and kick him out.

In our love, he gave me the gift of a beautiful daughter. In our marriage, he destroyed me and ground me down to the point that I was too broken to keep getting up, after being knocked down so often. He broke my spirit, my will.

This book is birthed out of the experience of an emotionally damaging marriage and the journey back to rediscovering self-respect, letting go of the hurt and hate I felt towards my husband, and finding forgiveness and compassion towards him. My husband only broke a part of me that was always fragile – my sense of self-worth. And his leaving gift to me was for me to heal myself and stand strong once again. I could hate him, but I don't. I will always love him, yet now it's from a far distance of safety – I will never forget his ability to hurt me.

He gave me my daughter and she is my true love of my life, my teacher and my motivation to be a better person. I wanted to be the mum that she so deserves. Being a lone parent hasn't been easy, being responsible for everything isn't easy. It's been hard financially, my career took a nosedive, my love of travelling has taken a bit of a diversion and my life has played second fiddle to my daughter's childhood. Are we happy, are we a strong little family unit? Yes, we are and that feeling is giving her the foundations for her to create the most amazing life for herself. One day I can sit back and watch her fly and know that I was a part of creating her strength and confidence – and that's what being a parent is all about.

I hope that in some way my experiences and journey are a comfort and support to you on your own journey. We are all unique and we can only hold a light out for one another. Ultimately, we must make our own choices based on our own inner wisdom as to how we parent, heal, move on. This book comes from my experiences and the choices that I made. It's my sincere hope that you can find comfort and some guidance from my words and remember: you are doing a fabulous job…

Much love

Trudy Joy

The Birth Of This Book

Have you ever had a feeling within you that felt bigger than you, a knowing and overwhelming feeling that you must act upon something unknown?

When I separated from my husband, after what had been a very destructive and abusive marriage, I needed something that would give me some hope, some optimism and a reassurance that my future and my life as a single parent was going to be okay. I needed to understand that I wasn't the only one who was feeling unsure and insecure – that I wasn't alone, sailing in the ocean of heartbreak and uncertainty. I wanted to read that someone had come through the worst of times and been able to create a positive, new, happily-balanced life for themselves and their children. I found websites geared towards single mothers to get some advice and while they were informative they were very matter-of-fact. Within the words, there was nothing that seemed personal, that you could connect directly too. I didn't read anything that gave me the warm inner glow of comfort.

In my early twenties, I experienced a spiritual epiphany, an awakening of sorts. Soon after this Divine revelation, I swapped my excessive partying lifestyle to hang out with the God men of India. I attended spiritual discourses, yoga classes and meditation retreats, to gain a deeper spiritual perspective. With my new realisations, I was drawn towards holistic healing, nutrition for vitality and vibrational medicine.

After a year or so of settling into my new reality as a single parent,

I was invited by a good and trusted friend, to a free event, where there would be a channelling with a spiritual master, known as Saint Germain. I'd never really heard of Saint Germain and was slightly suspicious of channelling, as I had never really experienced one before. It was one mile from my home, children were welcome, there was nothing to lose, it was 'donation only' and it would be something new with an unknown outcome. These were positive attractions for me. So, I went willingly along, with no expectation.

Let it be said that I was blown away and in awe of the amazing grace and love that flowed from Spirit through the medium. A Spirit Channel, or medium, has the ability to let a high vibration conscious energy take over his physical body, so that we can receive direct messages and love from the Divine Spirit. Saint Germain is an omnipresent master of wisdom, residing in the higher spiritual realms. Following my first group experience, I had an overwhelming inner feeling that I must book a one-to-one session, for a personalised channelling from Saint Germain. I had no idea why, yet the feeling was so strong that it had to be acted upon. It was in that meeting that the idea for this book came to light, as I was under strict instructions that I had to share my story.

I don't have narcissistic tendencies and found it incredibly challenging to be so open about something that seemed so personal. I had felt much shame during my marriage, the thought of having been so honest brought out a huge amount of resistance from within me. Making myself go public, so to speak, couldn't have been further from anything that I felt comfortable with. The idea of having to put together a whole book was overwhelming. My computer skills were basic, I had no idea where to begin with the 'story', or where to end, let alone what to put in the middle. I was newly-single, felt as though I was winging it in my life and really didn't think that I had anything to offer other parents in similar situations.

So, the book idea was put on the back burner and I carried on with my life. The idea of the project repeatedly niggled away at me. It felt as though it was something that I was meant to do – I just didn't know how. It took me months, even years, to begin to write anything worthy of publishing. Lots of small steps made up this journey. And with those small steps came great experiences, insight and learning from wonderful teachers, friends and events. With the experiences came wisdom, with the wisdom came the beginnings of mastering my life as a single parent. In my darker hours and as an unlikely answer to my prayers, I was given the task to write the pages that you see before you. As much as it is written to assist the reader, the healing and support that I received during this writing journey has been immense. As a result of re-living my past, I found inner happiness and peace with my marriage experience. Thanks to the Divine Grace it has been a beautiful, not easy, yet enlightening adventure, which has been surprisingly enjoyable. The end result has been to discover my true self through the process of self love, acceptance and forgivenss.

CHAPTER 1

Let Me Introduce Me

The Beginning of My Journey as a Single Parent

April 2008 was the last time my daughter and I saw her father. We didn't wave him goodbye, or wish him luck. There were no hugs. Instead I felt the final punch and I heard the last of his cruel comments and then he was gone.

I felt empty, exhausted and I hurt – I just hurt – from the outside all the way in. I hurt from the experience of having been a bruised wife. Maybe surprisingly I hurt for my ex-husband. I had known his softer side, I had loved him, our daughter had loved him. I just felt so remorseful for him, he had had everything. Regretfully his crazy temper destroyed our family and he walked away with nothing, apart from a broken heart. He walked away from his daughter whom he adored, his home and his UK life. He returned to his homeland, with nothing apart from a couple of bags and a few photos.

It was just so sad for all of us, but in amongst the emptiness I did feel relief: my marriage was the worst of times and thankfully those times had ended. I would no longer live trapped by fear, or having to live up to someone's ideals. My ex-husband's departure meant that I could begin to reclaim my freedom and identity. I could mother my daughter how I felt instinctively, rather than constantly being told what to do. Wow – I had freedom and it was huge and I no longer needed to walk on eggshells. I could stomp around like a great big flipping giant and no one was going to go into a fit of rage.

Many friends and family members were a little bit shocked and confused by my husband's swift exit from my life. They hadn't been privy to the dark inner sanctum of my marriage. It took a lot of energy explaining to people – partly because I didn't really want to identify with it, or to have to explain myself. I didn't want to break up my daughter's family, but there was no choice. My daughter needed to be raised in a safe, nurturing environment and we both needed to live in a free, happy and fun home. Living in fear of someone's temper: well, that's no life, as lost tempers can often have fatal consequences.

From those who didn't fully understand the extent of the violence and unhappiness during my marriage, I was accused of psychologically damaging my daughter, by instigating a physical separation between her and her father in her young, formative years. I was warned not to ask or expect any financial or other kinds of support. It really wasn't an easy time. I was already holding on to my own guilt, of my marriage failings. And with every time that I had to justify my actions, I felt worse. The remembrance of being a victim and having lost myself in the fear of domestic abuse was the place that I wanted to escape and run from.

Yet I still had to explain myself – they needed to understand that I wasn't calling time on my marriage on a whim. Of course, as they began to understand the extent of my plight, their opinions changed and I was given comfort and support that I desperately needed. During my ex-husband's wild rants, he would make threats and in his state of mind I believed him to be capable of anything at that time. Even though I knew that he had returned to India, my thoughts surrounding him were irrational. I was still looking over my shoulder constantly, double-bolting the door, locking the windows at night. I just lived with the unease that he was going to come back and carry out one of his threats. I still felt his judgment of me and even though he was physically 5000 miles away, his past actions and how I reacted were very much imprinted in my present. Those paranoid feelings slowly released their hold on me and we began to reconnect, mainly for my daughter and partly for me to forgive, let go and move forward.

The Abuse

Initially during the marriage I hadn't recognised myself as victim of domestic abuse. I associated domestic abuse with what's portrayed in television soap operas and mini-dramas. I hadn't been hospitalised with broken bones, I hadn't been pushed down a flight of stairs, or scalded with hot irons. I had just been the receiver of someone's violent temper and their cruel, vicious tongue.

My husband was the type of person who would always help a stranger, would always smile and have friendly chats with everyone he met – he was likeable. Due to his external disposition, I really could not understand how he could go from one extreme to another, and I always seemed to be the trigger for this sudden character change.

I was what's commonly known as being in a state of denial. I had been duped into believing that it was my fault and somewhere in my mind I began to believe that I deserved this treatment. Domestic abuse is a form of dark art: you are manipulated, dominated and controlled, almost as though your spirit and sense of self is being sucked out of you. It wasn't until later, when I researched domestic abuse that I really took ownership of the experience.

With my husband's growing frustrations and his inner deceptions growing, so did his anger and his verbal attacks turned physical. Kitchen knives were wielded at my throat, he would pull my hair harshly, suddenly, and hold it so tight that I couldn't get away. This behaviour became more regular and savage, the threats more terrifying, which were aimed at me, my family, our pets and any future that I may have aspired too. I can only say that by the grace of God, I was able to defuse the situation before I became a fatality. I suggested that he sought help and learn effective ways to manage and respond to his anger. He wasn't interested and insisted that I was the trigger and that it was my behaviour that had to change, not his.

Domestic abuse, or spousal abuse, can take its form in many guises. It may be sexual, physical, emotional or economic. It may be all four, as in my case, yet it's always about control. The abuser will use fear, guilt, shame and intimidation, which eventually wears you down. I often felt as though I was drugged by fear, I was zombified, I had no control of my life. I just felt utterly worthless and afraid to do or say the wrong thing that may invoke another angry episode. My ex-husband used his abusive behaviour to control me, he knew what he was doing. In the beginning, I really believed that I had made him angry and his abuse was just a kneejerk reaction to it. He would close all the windows, so that no one could hear what was about to be unleashed. He knew what he was doing. I was swallowing the abuse, I wasn't allowed to express the fear that I was feeling and if he caught me crying then I would again be screamed at for my weakness.

In lucid moments of realisation, many things went through my mind. How was this going to play out and how was this abuse going to end? Deep down I knew that things would continue to get worse, until the day the unthinkable happened. I had a choice: I could continue to stay in this very destructive relationship, or I could choose to get my life back on track. I had to end this destructive cycle. I owed a responsibility to my daughter, as well as myself. Once I had made my mind up to get out of this situation, I woke up one morning and I felt an overwhelming inner courage and strength. I don't know where it came from, I can only call it Divine Intervention. I could stand up for me, not in an aggressive way, it arose from an inner strength. This totally unnerved my husband.

The strength gave me a mental calmness, which was all I needed to see clearly and to find a way out of bedlam.

Maybe it was the fight or flight instinct taking over. He may have won the battles, but in the war to get my peace back, I was going to be victorious. My husband's UK spousal visa was expiring. I had no intention to renew it as his spouse, which meant that he had to step up or leave the UK. The timing luckily worked in my favour. I can't begin to explain the relief I felt. Looking back, I realise now, that I was in total denial as to the effects that the abuse had had on me.

My Daughter

My daughter was still young. As with any young child, they need a lot of love, attention and demand you to be present. Without her I could have ended up in an abyss of self-indulgent pity for much longer than would have been healthy. What I, we, had been through hadn't been the best of times. Yet we needed to move forward. By moving forward, the past experiences began to lose their power and I could make the practical changes that my new life as a single parent required.

Childcare was a necessity. I was a working mum and having debated taking some time out from my work to raise my daughter, I had to think what was best long-term. Investing my time in my daughter would have been wonderful, but financially I wasn't in a position to. State benefits weren't really an option. During our marriage, my ex-husband had racked up a lot of debt, mainly though bad choices and lady luck not being on his side. Due to the nature of our relationship, I had been bullied into providing him with money – money that I didn't have – so it was borrowed, which had left me responsible for repaying the creditors. So, I needed to keep with my job and work with that decision.

My mum flew in once again in her superhero ensemble, offering to have my daughter twice a week, leaving me just three days to find affordable childcare. Having done the math, I could afford a childminder rather than a private nursery. And so, the search began for the perfect child minder. Trusting in Divine Grace and my judgment I found the perfect lady, named Babs. Initially sending my daughter to be cared for by someone else didn't sit well with me. As her mum that was my job and I wanted to be the one she had fun with and would learn from.

In the beginning, she would cry every time I dropped her off and I would run out the door and sob. I felt so bad and guilty for abandoning her. She had been through so much already in her young life, just losing her father and now being left with strangers. I was however doing it for the right reasons, I was working to feed, clothe and house us, not because I was abandoning her. Thankfully she soon adjusted to her new routine. She was settled and looked forward to interacting with the other children and going on her little daily adventures with Babs and her child-minding crew. It was a huge relief to see her happy.

My mum and our childminder really cared for my daughter's wellbeing and both have been a hugely positive influence on her. The time that I then spent with my daughter was now special time. Partly down to the guilt of having missed many waking hours with her and because I wanted to hang out with her and be her mum. We didn't have a stereotypical routine for a child of her age – her bedtime varied depending on her tiredness. Play, cuddles, dinner, bath time and stories and bedtime cuddles was our routine. A routine with times set in stone didn't really come into the equation. Free flow worked well and it meant that I could have a waking relationship with her – after all that's what it's about.

As she grows and I age, our relationship together blossoms. Being just the two of us, our mother-daughter bond is very deep. It's not always plain sailing, I would like to meet a family where it was. I know that I really try my best as a mum and try to give her a happy and grounded childhood. I know deep down that I personally cannot fill the void of a father – it saddens me that she has that emptiness and that she misses the presence of a father. It's not always evident, yet the void within her does make itself felt on Father's Day and special occasions, or when we are on family days out and she is the only one without a father. It saddens me more that he doesn't really contact her or take an interest in her life, although maybe it's his state of mind, rather than him lacking in any love for her.

She often thinks it's her fault that her father and I are not together. Of course it's not and I reassure her that it's not. In her young mind she is trying to work out the marriage maths and coming up with a very unrealistic answer. It's common for young children to blame themselves, because they feel that inner rejection from the absent parent and can't understand why. They often don't understand that it's the parent and not them. I am honest with my daughter, without giving her all the gory details. I don't paint a faultless image of her father. She needs to understand that it is her father who is at fault and not her.

Part of my role as a single parent is to really be aware of how she is feeling emotionally. In this way I may support her in whichever way serves her best, so that her confidence and wellbeing continue to flourish. Surrounding her with as many positive role models, including lots of wonderful men, to help her to experience the male presence in her life. Much of the pain she is presently experiencing is caused I think by the lack of siblings in her life. There is nothing she would love more than a little sister or brother – it also pains me too. I feel a little inadequate because of her demands. I know that she would be an amazing older sister. How proud she would be. She has researched adoption and fostering. Our small flat is a bit too small for us and certainly wouldn't allow for more regular inhabitants. The size of our home also doesn't allow room for her other desire – pets or a small petting zoo. I don't give her false hope, but I do assure her that in the blink of an eye life can change. I have no idea what is around the corner. Neither does she. As long as we keep putting our wishes out to the mighty cosmos, and taking active and trusting steps, anything can show up at the right time.

My personal challenges

During my daughter's nightly bedtime cuddles, I would often doze off. My days were busy and sleep was a valued commodity. Often I would wake hours later to find the debris of dinner waiting to be cleared up, the general domestic chores that didn't magically disappear if I forgot about them. They were still there, ever-present and nagging. At that time life, with all its to-dos, felt relentless. Some evenings I would just feel completely overwhelmed. The transition from being married then not and becoming the all and everything to my daughter took some time to adapt to. Being the 'all' meant that I was the mum, the dad, the cook, the cleaner, the carer, the provider and plus a full-time worker. I was the one-hundred percent responsible parent. I felt like I was everything and nothing at the same time. When I became a mum, I lost me and had forgotten to put me back into the equation of my life. This was only amplified when I became a single parent.

Being a mum is an amazing experience and I cherished my daughter, but I felt as though I was running from A-to-Z, without being able to spend enough time with my little girl. My head was really jumbled. I was desperately trying to process what I had just been through and all the things that I had to sort out. Looking back now, I feel that I gave myself a hard time. As a mum, you give yourself ideals of how you would like to raise your baby. I felt I had failed her, because I had been duped into believing that I had failed as a wife. Yet reflecting now, I know that I had done everything I could to give her love. My non-work time was hers. She was always my number one, my priority.

Aside from adjusting to my newly-single status, I had to sort out the hangover caused from my ex-husband – and where to begin? The truth is I didn't really want to deal with anything. There had been such a lot going on and I was keeping my head above water, just. I didn't want to take responsibility of the debt and the way I was really feeling deep down inside.

My emotions were blocked up by an internal dam. Years of pushed down tears and held onto fears, upsets and injustices were all there, just waiting to be released. I knew it, I felt it. I just didn't want to own it. When I had to explain to folks how I ended up single, I could feel this knot in my throat. I could explain the story of being the abused wife and now the single mother by being totally detached, almost joking when I told them, as if it had happened to someone other than me. It was a crafted form of avoidance. Reflecting now, I realised that I didn't want people to see me as the victim that I had become. I didn't want them to see the hurt that was within. My transition into single motherhood was an uphill journey – there was a lot to deal with before I found the peace summit.

Becoming a mum is a big change. Becoming a single mum presents another set of challenges. Much of everything in life is about learning to survive the best way you can with new sets of circumstances. It's in these testing times that we grow as individuals.

CHAPTER 2

Getting My Life In Order

My Financial Flummox

After such a chaotic period of change, it was no surprise that I struggled balancing my finances every month. My paycheque would get gobbled up by credit card repayments, bills and loans. In a blink of an eye the money was gone. I was in a vicious circle with the money sharks chasing me around and around this never decreasing circle. I couldn't do more hours at work, as my job was salaried and there were no more hours on offer. Plus, I had a small girl needing me. And as much as she needed me, I needed her. I could have run away, I could have easily lost myself in hedonistic all-nighters. Her presence in my life made me face everything and will it to change, because as a parent I know, my actions are her teacher.

Airing my financial dirty linen just fills me with regret and irritation at having been so powerless to my ex-husband's demands. I had lost all my financial security, along with valued sleep, due to the twilight hour worries of how I was ever going to repay everything without resorting to selling my soul. I couldn't make sense of it, I just didn't know what to do. I felt desperate. The one thing that I did know was that I was going through a massive lesson. The first part of the lesson was to respect money by utilising it wisely. Secondly, never to lend anyone money that puts you at risk and thirdly respect your gut instinct. Remember, true love is free. Anyone who really loves you would respect your answer, whether it be yes or no, to their monetary demands.

I wasn't sure if love had clouded my judgment, or the fear of the consequences: probably both. I had to sort it out and take responsibility. I couldn't keep living with the stress, the stress of one day not being able to make the minimum payments, the stress of the bailiffs bashing down my front door and taking all my daughter's toys, my telly and my copper pots, in front of a street crammed with voyeurs. In my mind, I was in a worst-case scenario.

Eventually, surrendering to my ever-mounting stress, I began to research the option of debt management. Looking back, I should have spoken to an impartial party before signing on the dotted line. This was again another lesson learnt. I re-mortgaged what I could and with the remaining negative balance I sheepishly entered a debt management scheme. Getting into that much debt was a huge mistake and one I am still paying for. It amazes me that the banks at that time were willing to lend so much money, knowing the amount of my salary, yet that's another topic all together.

On the plus side, I have now become very money-savvy and have no desire to own a credit card or commit to a loan unless it's for a viable business purpose. After having been accepted and signing on the dotted line, I could relax, and the 'worst-case scenario' stopped playing out in my mind – my telly, daughter's toys and copper pots were safe. Joking aside I do live on a tight budget enforced by the terms of the debt management company. Also, we don't receive any childcare maintenance support from my daughter's father which is challenging, but not a surprise.

Our tight budget doesn't really allow for many, if any, luxuries. It was all about prioritising on the essentials. We got by, with a lot of juggling, shopping wisely, gratefully-accepted freebies, asking for help, taking advantages of sales and special offers, searching the rails of charity outlets, using retail gained points, wise Christmas and birthday suggestions and recycling. Having less cash forced my hand towards creativity, homemade cushion covers and blinds – my skill-base has probably grown by having less disposable income.

Making the best of my financial situation was the only way to keep going. Concentrating on the gifts and blessings that were in my life and being in a state of gratitude for them, rather than a mind-set of feeling lacking, worked wonders.

There are many things I have been unable to afford. Keeping up with financially secure married friends or single pals with no dependents was a race that I stopped taking part in. I soon learnt that you can only do what you can and there is no point in ever comparing yourself – financially or in any other aspect of your life – to another. Comparisons certainly don't lead to internal happiness.

I want to share with you also the amazing gifts that showed up whilst I was living on so little. I was gifted holidays by my parents, meals out from friends and family, unexpected presents. I received huge discounts on course fees and had medical bills paid. When I really needed something, then it would show up in the form of a generous gift. There were many times that I had no money in my pocket, my account would be empty and I would miraculously find a £20 note on the road side, which would buy enough food until payday. There were times when I would enter into an exchange of talents, instead of paying a cash fee. It was strange that when I stopped stressing about where the money would come from, it inevitably showed up. Amazing!

An Emotional Flooding

Returning to the story of the dam of emotions which was sitting undigested within me, sometimes you just have to break to allow yourself to be fixed. I am not exactly sure when my dam burst its banks – it certainly wasn't instantaneous after the separation. For many months I had been living on adrenaline, getting by and adjusting.

I remember sitting quietly one evening, whilst my daughter was sleeping, listening to a medley of tunes. A Coldplay song came on, aptly named "Fix You". The words haunted me to the depth of my core, triggering the release of a river of tears. The unfixed emotions of real heartbreak, failure, fear, betrayal, hurt, sorrow and the verbal bruises, rose to the surface. And that was the beginning of my healing journey. During the day I was mum and an employee and at night, when the house was quiet, I crumbled and morphed into a vulnerable human fountain.

When any significant relationship ends, you question the whys, the hows, as well as going through the motions of blame, guilt, anger, grief and eventually ending up at forgiveness. I had been emotionally bullied, mentally beaten and physically assaulted, and I couldn't understand how I had brought out such a venomous side in someone. I had always thought of myself as a strong character. I was kind and generally happy – had I deserved this treatment, had I done something wrong? I knew that I had tried and tried so hard to appease his demands.

I decided to pack myself off to weekly therapy sessions, with the hope of receiving some deeper if not profound insights, into the whys and hows. During the therapy sessions, I learnt to take responsibility for me and the role that I had played. I had not asked, nor had ever wanted, to be in such a dysfunctional marriage. Yet in letting myself become a victim to my ex-husband's anger, I had played 'submissive' very well. Love is a very strong motivator for staying with someone. It's my belief that everyone has a good and beautiful side to them, which is the side that you fall in love with. In my case, once I had fallen hard for the benevolent side it was a shock when this cruel, angry and vicious side came out. Wow, I never would have thought it would have been possible for my ex-husband to have such a crazed side to him. At times it was as if he relished his demonic personality and enjoyed tormenting me.

In the beginning, a big part of my therapy was to write pages and pages of inner blur. Every morning I would wake a half an hour early and begin to write everything, from feelings and thoughts, through to questions that popped into my mind. It was a mental purging of sorts. For six weeks I would write and write and write. Every wrong deed, hurt feeling, bitter remorse, anguish, dream, aspiration, desire and confused thought, I would write down. The idea behind writing pages is that you clear the clutter from your mind, so you achieve some clarity. It's private writing, no one is ever going to read it, which encourages you just to write whatever comes to mind.

In many ways the explanation that I had been looking for was self-love. If I had loved and respected myself more, would I have reacted to the warning signs earlier and walked away? The answer would of course be a 'yes'. Self-love is powerful, it creates a bulletproof bubble around you. I know that now. Yet at the time I wasn't putting myself first. Becoming aware of my own inner mental dialogue I realized that I was my own bully. For a long while it was easy to blame my ex-husband for all his wrongdoings and taking responsibility wasn't easy. The blessing that came from my marriage was of course our daughter. Apart from her, the experience had been a huge lesson in self-growth. I had survived and there must be something to be said for being a survivor.

Crushed Confidence

By the end of a turbulent few years, my confidence within was shot. My intuition of my husband had been completely off the mark, which meant that I found it difficult trusting my own judgment. On a scale of one to 10, I was cruising down the river on the number one boat, rapidly heading for the waterfall of 'I give up'.

I felt a mess, I felt frumpy. I felt wobbly and heavy. I didn't even really like me anymore, everything my husband had called me I had begun to identify with. Walking into new environments with new people wasn't a comfortable experience. I found it difficult to be myself, to open up and enjoy where I was. The lack of confidence made me feel nervous and shy in situations that previously I would have relished. When you feel confident, you feel invincible. I didn't feel like any superhero I had ever heard of. I often felt so passive and submissive, I did not stand up for myself. I just agreed to keep the peace, often getting trampled on in the process.

Luckily confidence is something that can be built up again, step-by-step. I surrounded myself with support and love – in many ways love and support came and found me. I began to start taking on board positive comments and to recognize the good qualities within myself.

Rebuilding confidence is quite a journey of self-discovery. I first had to look at my behavioural and thought patterns, and then begin to transform old habits. I devoted a lot of time to everyone else's needs and within that process managed to place myself way down in the pecking order. Replacing myself at the top, next to my daughter, was a big step in the right direction. Looking at the grey areas that I needed to shine a light on was the next step. Self-love was a massive task for me to get to grips with. Increasing my self-worth and valuing myself and my skills was another hurdle, and although I have arrived at a stage where now I have regained my confidence, the bugbears of fear and self-doubt do sometimes creep up on me.

When it came to learning new skills, however small or grand an accomplished goal was, it was honoured and celebrated. By focusing on the present and knowing that I would be walking towards a happier future, my confidence grew in my own abilities.

I sought out the right help, from the right people and even if it turned out they were the wrong people with the wrong advice, it helped me to value and hone my own judgement. I would put myself out there, having to face my fears, just to build up my shattered confidence. It wasn't comfortable and it was like opening a Pandora's Box of emotions and self-deprivation. I learnt how to handle rejection positively. Having faith in a greater benevolent power helped me to trust in myself and to accept things without judgement.

Support SOS

I have always been wildly independent. I like being unconstrained by others and situations and being self-reliant. But becoming a single parent has made me ask for help. I have had to become dependent on others' willingness to give me their helping hand, to survive. Not everyone can help when you need them to; everyone has their own lives. Sometimes I have really needed childcare help and it hasn't been there and at those times it has felt like I am alone, desperate and isolated. People support in many different ways: they support when and where they can and how they know. My mum and dad help with holiday childcare and school pick-ups. My parents have both been there for financial SOS moments, when the boiler packed up, the car got pranged, and when I ran out of money to buy my daughter a winter coat. My sister and her husband make every effort to include my daughter in their family unit. Friends have been the ears, the play and the laughter. I am grateful for what they each do individually in helping me cope.

I found that being a single parent limits my freedom, in all kinds of aspects of my life I didn't expect – from candidly chasing my dreams or just popping out for an evening jog. Not having a husband at home to help as a husband or father would, specifically with the childcare, meant that I felt really trapped in my flat. My job covered the bills and the hours suited my life. In many ways, I was lucky to be in that position and I know that. Especially that I got on with my employer and the team. There were no future long-term prospects and therefore long-term security. I really needed to retrain to be able to give myself another career path and a way of security for the future. I may well meet Mr Right 'forever' one day, but that doesn't mean that comes with any financial security either.

Presently I am the provider for myself and my daughter. And this world isn't getting cheaper, with monetary demands escalating annually. Retraining was something that I felt I really needed to do, to be able to give myself and my daughter more financial security and to open the door to new experiences. I hit a road block with no childcare help on offer, I felt overwhelmingly trapped and sad with frustration. Being a single parent felt like a huge great block to my future.

You can't leave young children without care and you can't always get care due to limited cash flow (well I couldn't) and having to repay childcare favours can just add to the daily pressure. Having the freedom to pop out to attend a course became a mission. I felt the tick-tock-tick of my life and whereas I don't like to put an age limit on things, retraining doesn't just happen overnight, nor does establishing yourself in a new career. It was and will always be important to me.

To study and retrain all boiled down to finding willing support. I put a group email out to my nearest and dearest asking for help, so that I may attend college 10 weekends a year. Spread out over the year no one became burdened by my needs and my daughter got fun days away from mum with an assortment of her favourite people. Being a lone parent has made me step off my independent soap box and ask for help when I have needed it, because asking for help is the only way to get ahead.

Loneliness

Loneliness is a strange emotion. There are times in our lives that we can enjoy being by ourselves. I for one crave a healthy dose of solitude and rather than viewing it as being lonely, it is space to just be. There are other times when we can feel so alone, yet be surrounded by people. Loneliness is a result of how we are feeling within, rather than external conditions. These can include feeling isolated, friendless, rejected and excluded. I went through times of loneliness; sometimes it felt extreme. The rest of the world was turning, but I was in my little flat alone at night, whilst my young daughter slept. Little young ones don't talk – though there is of course some level of communication – and I missed the adult interaction. During my marriage I was lonely, because I felt so rejected, by my husband and myself.

In the early years of my single mum time, I did feel that I was held in nightly solitary confinement at the beck and call of my daughter's needs. I felt as though the freedom of my youth was far behind and I missed that freedom. I wanted to socialise occasionally, yet my funds were already stretched and paying for a babysitter was an additional expense. My little flat was quite small, too small to hold any type of gathering comfortably. My job too was quite isolating. Being lonely often meant that I had no real release. Problems churned around my mind, having a rolling snowball effect. I felt emotionally heavy, bored and really began to question my life's purpose. After all, the world was still turning and I didn't appear to be turning with it. My nightly mates became chocolates and biscuits. I created my very own 'sweet life', my very own Willy Wonka experience. I became a secret twilight muncher. Not a great habit, it certainly didn't bring me any long-term joy. My jeans got tighter and my heart got heavier. The sugar sent me to cloud happy, then crashed me down onto the rocks of sadness and self-disgust. I think it is probably defined as emotional eating for comfort, but momentary comfort. I really missed not having a loved one to chat to. As strange as it may seem after all the drama my ex-husband created, we had had a great friendship. His unbalanced side hadn't been a permanent feature in our relationship, especially not in the beginning. Although I felt a lot of relief at his departure, I really missed the friend I had in him. I wish everything was black and white but it's not. I wasn't a hermit. Friends and family would pop over and I would go out with my daughter in tow, yet in the main I was home alone.

As I began to accept my life, I started to develop new interests and hobbies, as a healthier and more positive alternative to eating myself to short bursts of happiness. I started to learn new things to gain a different perspective on life. I watched inspiring documentaries, read books, joined groups, attended talks and courses, and just began to be passionate about learning. Much of my learning was for self-inquiry. Being a chef and having an affinity for creating tasty morsels, when I felt the onset of frustration or stress, I would go to the kitchen and play around with new culinary ideas. Cooking became my meditation and a creative outlet. The empty boredom was filled and the loneliness banished.

A 'Depressed and Stressed' Cocktail

Put the ingredients of loneliness, bad diet, lack of exercise, heartbreak, financial pressure and abuse recovery together and top it off with being the responsible one – is it any wonder that I slid down the dark hole into a depressed state? Of course not. I was coming from being in a dark relationship and my inner happiness barometer hadn't been high for some time. Please don't misunderstand me, my daughter, friends and family made me happy, and the unexpected beauty of life often bought a tear to my eye. I am speaking of the inner heaviness of recent experiences and my life not having turned out the way that I had hoped. The life I was living certainly wasn't the one I wanted the starring role in. In fact, it sucked for a period, and I gave myself a hard time for it. I was depressed and in a negative state of mind: I couldn't find 'happy' because I couldn't see a way out.

I was prickly with stress and emotionally oversensitive. This was not a good feeling and I was probably not the easiest person to be around. Sometimes it takes someone else to kick your butt into reality and I got that collective kick from many angles. And I had to make the changes by taking responsibility for how I was feeling.

Fear of the Future and Being
Unsatisfied in the Present

I found when I first separated from my ex-husband, I felt a huge amount of relief. Our new day-to-day routine had fallen into place beautifully. We were reclaiming some balance and peace, and ultimately, I felt so much happier. I began to take responsibility for the emotional and financial grey areas, left behind from the marriage. Everything really was going in the right direction. And then I felt as though I hit a brick wall of realisation – that this was it, well, my life for a while. Staying in night after night, doing the domestic chores, going to work, taking care of my daughter and not achieving anything other than surviving the day-to-day.

I really lost the light, fun perspective of life. I felt incredibly unsatisfied in the present, with everything that I had, and I put this down to fearing the future. I felt as though I didn't have any future financial security. I was living on a squeakily tight budget. I couldn't understand or make any sense of how this was going to change in my current situation. As a parent, you know that your life is busy and you also have financial responsibilities, as well as the upbringing of your children. Risking the security that you do have can feel like a gamble with an unknown outcome. As a lone parent the buck starts and stops with you. There isn't the support or back up of a partner, who can assist financially or with childcare, or that you can work as a team with, to make changes to your family's life. It's a different reality and can make you feel as though you are out bobbing in the big blue ocean all by yourself.

When you are living close to your financial edge, as I really was, just being able to make ends meet monthly was a pressure. Living this way had become a habit. I was really living in fear of lack of money. Due to this mind-set, I really worried about the future, how was I going to upgrade to a bigger home, pay for university fees, go abroad, study – you name it. Anything with a price tag on it popped into my mind.

At the same time, it appeared that I was surrounded by those who, outwardly at least, seemed to be soaring in success in every aspect of their lives. Whilst I felt as though someone had pressed the 'pause' button. I wasn't necessarily deeply unhappy, but I did question my life and my ability to make changes.

The fundamental problem was, I was missing the point. I had a roof over my head, we had food in our fridge, we had clothes on our backs, and we were safe, warm. Millions in this world have a lot less. We had everything we really needed in that moment of our lives. I could spend time with my daughter and that really was and is the most important thing. I began to change my perspective, to being grateful for all that I had. And from this powerful stepping stone, I also began to be grateful for all the things that I had accomplished and the obstacles I had overcome.

Often, we cannot see or recognise our achievements, or spot our talents. It can take a loyal friend to see the potential that you have within you and point it out. These reminders are so beneficial, it's easy to get lost in the struggle and forget yourself and all that you are. Focusing on me a little more gave me the confidence to believe that "Yes, even though I was single parent, I could still carve out a future." In that renewed head space, I began to focus on what I wanted to do and to work out the steps that I would need to take to get there. Breaking goals down into doable phases is a good place start.

My 'X Factor Anger' issues

If I have said that I had been unaffected by my ex-husband's behaviour towards me, I would be a liar. It's one thing to know and accept something is over and move on. It's another thing to accept 'the way' the relationship ended – i.e. the reasons for the breakdown of a marriage. It's often the path of events leading up to 'D-day' that have caused the pent-up emotions. Every divorce, every break-up, has its own unique story and some stories are thankfully amicable, whilst others are not. For those that are not, there is need for healing and letting go. The feelings of the emotions should be acknowledged, otherwise they sit within us like a rotten egg. It becomes the white elephant that we take with us into every new relationship journey that we embark on.

I have been honest in the sharing of my own experiences. I have mentioned the sadness I felt, the shame. Until now I have failed to mention the anger I felt towards my ex-husband. I was angry at the way he had controlled me with his anger and violence, cheated on me, belittled me, stole from me, the endless lies. I was angry at myself for being so gullible, for being so sucked in. I felt cheated by his deception. I was angry that I was left alone to be a single parent, with so much that needed to be sorted out. My life had become harder than I had ever imagined that it would have been and I didn't like it. And it was his fault. It felt as though he really didn't care. It infuriated me that he hadn't wanted to try to deal with his anger issues, that he would rather give up on our family. I felt angry that he walked away from our future, and our daughter, so easily. I know now, of course that isn't that case, and I am aware that he feels a tremendous sadness from not being with his daughter. He simply wasn't ready to deal with the secret pain that he carried around with him. He wasn't willing to deal with it, to save our family unit. I wanted his good side back for good, I wanted his mental unbalance to remedy itself. I wanted the man I had fallen in love with to return.

Anger is not a healthy emotion to walk around with. It unbalances your wellbeing, clouds your judgment, creates stress and destroys your peace of mind. Your thoughts can become vengeful and obsessive. You may choose to stay angry at a person because you may believe that they deserve the anger for how they seemingly wronged you. In the long-term the only person you are really harming is yourself. Anger often is a mask for sadness and when you let the anger go, you uncover the real sadness. I processed my anger by writing it out, by talking, by taking responsibility and forgiving. Forgiveness doesn't mean forgetting. It also doesn't mean that you must accept a repeat pattern of the behaviour either. Forgiveness just sets you free from the attachment. It's making a choice to let go and move forward with freedom.

The Remedy to Bouncing Back

Acceptance and happiness are the key to life! When you are happy, life flows, obstacles can be overcome with ease. Your whole mind-set is different. Happiness really helps to detach from outcome, because the feeling of true happiness comes from within.

My remedy to finding happy began by treating my life as a whole. And learning to love myself. For one thing to work well, every aspect needed to work, so that mine and my daughter's lives flowed. Finding happy for me was to start with accepting my life and owning all that it was. I had to take responsibility for making our life work, with what we had at our disposal and what I could add to it, to make it better. And that is exactly what I did. It hasn't been easy, but what is easy? I still do have challenging days. I do get frustrated with the lack of time, money, freedom and there to are those days when I feel as though I am walking up a very steep hill. Thankfully these days pass. I feel blessed to have my daughter. We have a unique and beautiful relationship. We can drive each other crazy at times. Hand on my heart, I can say that it has been beyond a privilege to have had this one-to-one time with her. I feel excited for her life and I feel excited for our life too.

No one knows what the future really holds for any of us. I've learned a few things along the way that helped me 'to look on the bright side of life'. When you get knocked down, you get up and you keep getting up. Life knocks even those whom seemingly have everything. It's life's way of teaching us to recognise our inner strength and what is truly important. Seize new opportunities that come your way and don't allow the past to stand in the way of new possibilities. Equally so, don't let your own or others limiting thoughts about yourself hold you back. Where there is a will, there is a way – and where there is a way, there's hope.

Everything is possible. There is a solution to everything, even if it is not immediately apparent. Something deemed impossible changes when someone does the impossible. Self-judgment is a waste of energy, self-improvement is where the gold lies. Don't put yourself under too much pressure with unrealistic demands on your time and take time to have fun, to love and nurture yourself and your family. Every time you feel low and in a negative head space about yourself or your life, do something positive, that reaffirms to you and the universe that you deserve love and happiness. Life is for living and everything has the potential to be transformed. When you tap into your true spirit, you will know that you can achieve all that you want to and you will understand that you are a co-creator of your life, not merely a participant or passenger.

CHAPTER 3

Becoming A Single Parent

I t's new, it's unfamiliar and as with many things that we haven't previously experienced, it can feel daunting. Naturally it will bring up our inner insecurities about our ability to parent alone. We live in a world where the ideal belief has always been 'mother-father' parenting, although this is often not the case these days. Being a lone parent doesn't fit everyone's archetype. Yet archetypes are having to change, as society evolves and pushes the boundaries of previous set ideals. And the circumstances of every case of single-parentage are not the same.

There is no denying that it takes a male and female form to create life. That is the magical natural polarity/mystery of life. Yet parenting is love and nurture, and one parent can successfully bring up a child, or children even. The challenges you face will be different, it's true, yet the foundations for successful parenting are the same.

As many, I didn't set out on the parenting journey alone. However, I would be the first to raise my hand every time to be a lone parent, rather than endure an unhappy and fearful marriage. So here I am and here you are, and instantly we are no longer alone. And so too are hundreds and thousands of parents, just like us, experiencing this journey as single mums, single dads, and guess what? Their world and ours is still turning. A child or children can be raised perfectly well with one strong, balanced and responsible parent. And they too can grow up to be strong, happy and successful beings.

Relationship Crossroads. Which way to go...?

This can be an onerous time. The concluding decisions you and your partner make are going to change the reality for you and your family. Walking away from a marriage or relationship is never easy, especially when children are involved. It is a decision that really needs to be given time and respect. You must feel that you have tried everything that you can in your power to make the relationship between you and your partner work. If after all your efforts nothing has noticeably changed, then something is wrong. The spark of happiness and love needs to be alive for a partnership to succeed. Every relationship can go through trying times. Yet after the bumpy spell, happiness should return. In a partnership there should be trust, love and respect. You should feel safe and content in each other's company and you should both be working towards your family's collective happiness. If you are not able to reach this space, letting each other go – so that you may make a new happiness – is the fair thing to do.

If you have experienced any type of abuse in your relationship and don't feel that your home is a safe place for you or your child, it is time to move on before the abuse becomes worse. If you are living in fear, then there are organisations which can help you. They can offer refuge for you and your children, giving you a safe base and remove you from any immediate harm. Confide in someone. Once you can open up about the abuse, then you are admitting to yourself that something is wrong and something needs to change. It's a positive step, the first one you can take. You don't deserve to be abused – period! You know what a good marriage is, you know how people should treat each other. Don't let low self-esteem, or being bullied, keep you stuck in a relationship that doesn't serve those ideals. If your partner suffers from anger issues, they are their issues and they need to take responsibility for them. Life is too short to be a verbal or physical punching bag. Take responsibility for your happiness and your freedom. Ask for help, because you deserve better, despite what you may inwardly be feeling. You deserve better.

Sometimes relationships come to a natural end. Some partners we have in life give us experiences that help us grow and learn, but their presence in our lives may not be a permanent feature. When married or in a committed relationship, the desire is that mutual love is everlasting. Some relationships are destined for longevity, while others are not. Everything is unique. The world we live in is unique.

At the crossroads, in your heart you will know if separation is the right thing to do. It's in that knowing you will find the courage to move forward. Staying together for the children isn't really a viable option, unless you can put your differences aside and live harmoniously with one another. Children don't need to live in a hothouse, they also don't need to see their parents behaving negatively towards one another. Children are like sponges, absorbing so much of what goes on around them, often mimicking the behaviour they have learnt in their later adult relationships.

Doubt is a very common symptom caused from any forthcoming change. If you know your relationship isn't working, yet you still feel there's hope, try a trial separation. This will help to clarify any niggling doubts that you and you partner may have. Maybe you just need some space for a while. Try counselling, together and separately, to work on your own individual issues. Spend some time each day focusing on what you really appreciate about them. Write a list and reflect upon it, adding something new each day. During intimate relationships, life can get in the way, with all that it throws at us. And we become attached to the unfolding dramas and we lose the focus to keep that flame, that spark of love, fully ignited. We forget, we get amnesia. If you are on or considering a separation, take time to remember, to forgive and let go of hurts that got you to the point where you are now. You are working towards a new beginning, whether that is together or separately.

A friend of mine repeatedly says to me "You need to be brave to get a divorce" and I agree with her. Initially it's a bumpy ride, as you try to find your footing on a new path, but with the right help and support you will get your groove back and create a new life for yourself and your children. With fresh beginnings there are new opportunities, on so many levels. Every path away from the difficult decision of the crossroads offers a new beginning. It's important not to judge yourself: a failed marriage began as a success, it's just that the love ran out somewhere along the line.

Being a Lone Parent from Conception

Through choice or through unforeseen circumstances, you may be commencing the parenting journey alone. Pregnancies can be unexpected and not always greeted favourably by both parties. It happens and it hurts when you are with someone and they don't want to play happy families with you. It's a painful kick to the heart. We aren't always ready to be parents at the same time.

It will be completely natural for you to feel overwhelmed and apprehensive. You may doubt your own parenting abilities to raise a child, from the word go, alone. Let the feelings come up in you and talk to a trusted friend or family member, or a councillor, about your concerns. You will need support, as it is this support that will give you the momentum for the belief in your parenting abilities to grow. So that you begin to feel confident in your new role as a mother or father.

Having a child is amazing and it's so important that you enjoy the pregnancy process and that you are in a positive state of mind to make the best choices for you and your growing child. If the pregnancy is totally unplanned, then you will need time to get your head around the imminent changes. You will wonder how a child is going to fit into your life, how you will cope, how you will make it work and whether you're ready for it. You have nine months to adjust to the idea of becoming a parent. The best advice that I can offer you is to use this time wisely.

Create a circle of support of your nearest and dearest. They can help you through the birth, the arrival and to be there for you. You will need rest. Parenting a new born is exhausting. Doing it by yourself means that it all falls at your feet. The more people that are willing and committed to help you and your little one, the easier you will find it. Nature made babies too cute to resist. It's an honour for most people to play a starring role in a new-born's life. Babies bring a sense of wonder with them. But don't be afraid to ask for help. If you are met with resistance and those around you are a little concerned that you are alone and pregnant, their resistance will change when the baby comes along. Babies have the ability to melt hearts and their presence in a family can bring great joy to everyone.

On a very practical note, work out your finances so you know where you are money-wise and you can draw a realistic budget. Prepare for the baby's arrival. Buy the things you need gradually over the pregnancy period. Of course, you will receive gifts. If people are asking and willing to help contribute to the baby fund, then ask for the things that you will need. Create a favourites list on a supermarket delivery site, so that all you need to do is press go and your groceries will arrive stress-free. Stock your home with non-perishables and homemade prepared frozen meals. Cooking is the last thing that you need on your mind, but this way you are eating nutritious healthy home cooked meals that will support your body. You'll find more on diet and healthy living later in this book.

Research how you would like to raise your child. There are many different parenting methods and some can be conflicting, so choose one that you feel comfortable with. These nine months are all about the preparation and bonding with your baby. You need to enjoy being a parent. Your little baby will need you to be in a happy place. Get your birthing team around you and attend birthing classes and prenatal yoga classes if you can. Use this time to meet other new mothers. After your baby is born, join mother and baby groups, and toddler groups, where you can make lasting and genuine friendships with other new mums. These are great ways of meeting other mothers and forming strong friendships for you and your child. Being a lone parent can be quiet isolating. Babies don't talk, they demand your attention. Getting out of the house and connecting with other new mothers and sharing stories and receiving advice can be really beneficial.

I remember when my daughter was born, she was so little and perfect. Her physical arrival into the world was like the excitement I would feel as a child, when Santa had fulfilled my Christmas wishes, yet a million-fold. Such an amazing, exciting and joyful time. When the child arrives it's as though all the fear and doubt just melt away. You are still you, possibly a more selfless version of yourself. The biggest difference is that now you are with a plus one. If you are doing it alone now, it really doesn't mean that you will be alone forever. Life takes us all on funny twists and turns, and often, life doesn't go how we planned.

Parenting Goes on After a Bereavement

One of the cruellest acts of fate is when your beloved is taken from this world too prematurely. Whether it is a terminal illness or a freak accident, their departing is far too soon. It is immensely heart-breaking, for you and the whole family, for so many reasons. It's not just at the space that their parting has left in your life, in your family's life. It is far deeper. Your joint dreams go with them too and you are left feeling that your future has been stolen from you.

If your partner died from a terminal illness, you may have had time to mentally adjust and prepare for life without them. A sudden death is a tremendous shock. It's so sudden that you almost go into autopilot, surviving purely on adrenaline. You're supporting your kids through this difficult phase, trying to process what has happened – to have suddenly become both mum and dad – and having to consolidate the combined day-to-day chores. Whichever way you lost your partner, your husband, your wife, your best friend, soulmate, your beloved, death is still death and it's so sad to lose someone you loved so dearly.

Grieving is an important process to go through. You must acknowledge everything that your beloved represented to you. You have to cry. Your kids need to see you cry too, so that you can all grieve together. You don't need to be the rock, you may feel like you do, but you don't. Let your friends and extended family be strong for you, whilst you come to terms with the loss. Give yourself as much time as you can to adjust to being a single parent.

Friends and family will also be missing them, so speak with them regularly for support and comfort. They may be able to spend time with the children, so that you can have some alone time, to process your feelings, enabling you to adjust to the shock of losing someone you loved so dearly. Most people will be very compassionate and go out of their way to help you. If help is offered, accept it. It is offered to you as their way of showing their respect and offering their condolences. It's often hard to find words to console a broken heart and in many cases actions speak louder than words. If you are struggling, then you must speak to someone who has insight into bereavement and can offer you practical and supportive advice, so that you may make the transition. Life does move on, but it doesn't mean that you should forget them. A beautiful idea is to honour them annually by fulfilling one of the 'to do' dreams that you once shared. It's important for your children too. They also need to know and understand what the departed parent was like and in a way, it keeps their memory alive.

How to Go About Getting a Divorce

If you have decided that as a married couple or civil partnership you need to separate, you have only one option. Getting a divorce is relatively easy in the UK – if you are both in agreement as to the reason for the divorce, how you will look after the children and how you will split up the money, the property and your possessions. You can do it by yourselves, without the need for solicitor representation. If there are any grey areas, it feels complicated, or you feel that you need to clarify certain areas, then it is very advisable to use a divorce specialist to assist or represent you. Your solicitor will be representing you, making sure that you get the best financial and custody settlement for you and your children. In some divorces cases, the marriage breakdown may have resulted in a bitter feud. Where there are volatile and heightened emotions, it is strongly advisable to involve a mediator, who can deal with things rationally and calmly. If you are a low-income family, you may be able to receive legal aid – many legal firms offer this as an option. It will be assessed on proof of earnings.

To get a divorce in the UK you will have needed to have been legally married for over one year and be a fulltime resident in the UK. You must agree with your spouse that the marriage relationship has permanently broken down. The first step is to file a divorce petition. For this you need to apply to your local county court for permission to divorce, by submitting a divorce petition. You must explain the reasons why you are divorcing. The reasons can include unreasonable behaviour, physical abuse, verbal abuse, drunkenness or drug-taking or refusing to pay for housekeeping. Other options include adultery, if your husband or wife is having a sexual relationship with a third party. But you may not give this reason if you have continued to live with your partner for six months after the betrayal. You can also cite desertion (your wife or husband has left without your agreement and without good reason, for more than two years, to end your relationship), you have lived apart for two years and your spouse agrees to the divorce, or you have lived apart for more than five years and your spouse doesn't agree.

You will also need to fill in an additional form for your children, if they are under 16 years old, or under 18 and still in education. You will need to include arrangements for childcare, maintenance and contact with the children. The initial court fee will be approx. £500 (2017) when you start the divorce proceedings. If you are on benefits or low income you may be able to get help with the court fees and receive legal aid.

After you have submitted the 'divorce petition' and the 'arrangement for children' paperwork, if you and your ex-partner agree about the divorce petition, you can then apply for the Decree Nisi. After six weeks, you may then apply for a Decree Absolute, the legal document that signifies the end your marriage. It can feel like a very sad day when it falls through your letter box, as it marks the official ending, and it can reawaken those feelings of regret. Honour and acknowledge how you feel, but there is no need to dwell. What has happened has happened and you cannot undo the past. Learn from it and move on. All the forms are available to download on gov.uk. When contacting the county court, you need to speak with the family division. You do need to keep the Decree Absolute, as you will need this to show your marital status for official purposes. You will also need to produce it if you plan to remarry in the future. As well as marking the end of your marriage, the arrival of the Decree Absolute can also feel like a welcomed new beginning to a happier new phase of your life.

Compassion for the Ex

Every separation is unique. For whatever reason something ends, whether it's a mutual decision or not, there is heartbreak. I have mainly focused on you, the main carer of the kiddies, as that's what I know and can relate to. Let's just for a moment talk about the one who doesn't get to have the kids at home all the time, the one who has to move out of the family pad immediately, into their new reality.

When I grew up my perspective of marriage was mainly influenced by the American TV soap operas Dynasty and Dallas, where there was a lot of infidelity, mainly by the men who easily moved on and didn't really look back. But these are heartless characters. Most human beings have an emotional heart and I naively believed that all marriages failed due to men and their roaming eyes and wandering hands. I also came from a family where all the adults in my parents' generations had separated and ultimately divorced, so my views on marriage where rather pessimistic. Sure, some marriages end due to infidelities, but in many cases, it's just about that cup of love being empty, everything has been done and tried to keep those fires of love and passion alive. When it's time to move on, it's time to move on. It's sad, but true.

Over the years, I have met many men whose wives have initiated the separation for whatever reasons. But these heartbroken men are gutted and the first couple of months in their new, often much smaller homes, can be massively lonely and incredibly quiet, without the noise of their children, and quite bare without the family clutter. Adjusting to the new environment is not easy and it takes time to settle into the new phase. Be patient with them, try and let go of the reasons behind the separation and show compassion. Allow access to see the children regularly and routinely, both for the sake of the children and your ex. Communicate with compassion and try to find some friendly ground.

Your ex may move on quickly, because some men don't like being alone, whilst another's fear of rejection may hinder him from searching out new love. If you have found new love quickly, just be compassionate to how this may affect your ex. Be considerate and maybe give it some time before parading them around. Some men may feel a bit replaced, especially if they are in the new home with their kids. Over time, everything gets easier. Just give patience and show compassion to how others are feeling.

CHAPTER 4

The Modern-Day Pressures Of Being A Parent

Being a mother, a father, a parent, is the most important job in the world and probably the hardest – although admittedly not the most dangerous. It is a role that has been sadly undervalued in the western world for such a long time. Spiritual teachers and ancient wise folks of the world have recognised the importance of a mother/father and the need for good parenting within a child's life. Both the positive and negative influence a parent has in raising their child will form the world's societies. We, as parents are presently raising the next generation, a generation whom can continue to help make sizable and positive changes to world society, helping our home planet to become a more peaceful and a balanced place to live. What we invest in our children is never wasted. Raising a child with love and nurture, teaching them values and morals, showing them that there are consequences to actions and most importantly installing a strong belief of self-worth and courage into a child's being are paramount to the way that child will react and interact with society. Yet it takes time and patience to raise a child, something which modern living doesn't always permit.

A child will learn so much from the way he or she has been interacted with at a young age. They are little sponges, soaking up everything. If they are shown love, patience and kindness they in turn will reflect this out into the world throughout their lives. If they are ignored, shouted at, controlled and criticised, they will retreat within themselves, afraid to show the world who they really are, because they feel worthless. Raising a child is such a worthy investment of your time. Mother and fatherhood is a role that should be honoured and respected above all other roles in this world. Children need love and proper guidance.

Governments are very keen to get parents back into the workplace, earning taxable money. With the increasing pressures and mounting costs of living in a modern society, women often have no choice other than to return to work while the children are still young. I know I did. It's only a handful of mothers who have joyfully returned to work, whilst letting someone else care for their child. It's not a bad thing to return to work if you are in a career that fulfils your ambition, as you bring the positive energy home with you. Being a full-time mum isn't for everyone, you should do what suits you or what you need to do. I feel as though I missed so much of my daughter's young years, that when I was not at work, I choose to always be there for her.

There are huge pressures on mothers. The media, through advertising and film have created the ideal mother to be a size zero, wrinkle-free, immaculately dressed, a multi-tasking success story, juggling motherhood with a booming career, and a full and busy social life filled with equally glamorous and gorgeous people. All this, while living in a pristine mansion. And it's not to say that you can't have it all, but for me there aren't enough hours in the day to maintain this lifestyle, unless I had a team of paid assistance helping with the childcare, the housekeeping and running my life. It's an unrealistic expectation, and only a small percentage of the world's population can maintain this media-created 'ideal' life style. It would be amazing and comforting if motherhood was portrayed with a little more realism, for those of us who are not in the minority. Yet I guess it is something to aspire to.

The spirit of parenting is simply love, a very consuming and selfless love. It's not about living up to media ideals and being a super successful superwoman/superman, it's about being a super mum or dad to your kids. Providing your family with what they need. Mother and fatherhood is all about love and nurture, a role that deserves a lot more respect than it is currently given in the modern world we live in.

The Negative Stigma That Surrounds Single Parents

In the past, single parenting was really surrounded by negative connotations. As times have and continue to change, so too have these judgmental perceptions. I imagine a lot of these were brought about from religious ideals and the views of sex out of wedlock. A child born out of wedlock with no father present bought shame upon the family. Girls were forced into having abortions, or were sent away for the pregnancy and the child was taken away, which was very traumatic and deeply heart-breaking. Keeping the baby, tainted the reputation of the mother. These women were often cast out from society by the good God-fearing folk, who believed that sex before marriage was a sin.

People's judgments can be cruel, unkind and misguided. In recent times, single mums have been blamed for the problem children, the downfall of society. There are thoughtless articles written in nameless newspapers, which are written from solely a place of judgment and with the lack of empathy and compassion. Single parents can be seen as benefit-grabbing layabouts, whom just breed for government handouts and free homes. Yet the reality is that it is hard to live on benefits. They don't go very far. Therefore, is it fair to cast such aspersions? In general, those who are on benefits are on them for necessity rather than out of choice. Approximately 47% of children in single parent homes live in relative poverty. In the UK today (2017), there are around two million single parent families, 67% of which are in work.

There is a different stigma that surrounds single fathers. Single fathers made up 13% of the single parents in the UK. Single fathers do an amazing job, but there is no real recognition or acknowledgment of them and many support groups are aimed specifically at single mothers. Fathers in society are often seen as the disposable parent when it comes to divorce and custody of the children. Yet their presence, and the importance of their role within the family unit, should really be valued and honoured.

The positive truths of living as a single parent are often overshadowed. The strength of character, the dedication to the child/children, the sacrifices made, the desire for the survival of the family unit, they are all present. The pressures single parents are under today are enough, without negative labelling.

Most single parents didn't ever start out with the desire to raise a child solo. Like many others, I dreamt of a lasting relationship, a house filled with laughter and happiness, of being part of a loving and committed family unit. Sadly, that illusion shattered very early on in my own marriage and time was called on that dream. There are those who start off the parenting journey alone through choice. With modern day fertility procedures, it is possible to become a parent by yourself with the help of donation, because they haven't met the right partner, yet desire to have a child. Whether it is through choice or unforeseen circumstances, raising a child alone doesn't deserve anything less than healthy admiration and compassion.

Why There Are Rising Numbers of Single Parents in Modern Times

In the 2016 UK census, it showed that there are approximately 2 million single parent families in the UK. Meanwhile in the USA, the number of children being raised by a single parent is 12 million, a figure that has nearly doubled in 50 years. Most single families are headed by women.

Life in the 21st century is stressful. We are often chasing our tails trying to balance finances, jobs, successfully raising children, and worldly commitments. We get on each other's nerves because we are stressed. We forget to react from the heart. Hurt feelings grow, manifesting in anger and sadness.

Our relationships require work – they are living, breathing entities that need nurturing and communicating. The ring on the finger does not have magical properties that can hold a marriage together. The vows that are taken during the marriage ceremony need to be acted upon and honoured, to give them a depth of meaning rather than just empty words. Often, we forget why we fell in love, we forget the little things about that person that made them stand out from the thousands of others. We forget what it was that made them so dearly special to you. The combination of all these things diverts us on a different path, which can ultimately lead us to the divorce courts and to becoming another statistic.

It is not just divorcing parents that have led to the increase in numbers of single families. Many couples choose not to marry and so therefore are seen as single parents, even though they are living very contentedly under the same roof. Same-sex couples are included in the above statistic, because of the legalities of marriage, yet they too can be living very harmoniously as a family unit. Families whom have suffered from bereavement are also grouped into this statistic. All are classed as single parents.

CHAPTER 5

The Obstacles Faced By A Lone Parent

Firstly, with every obstacle there is a solution – obstacles can be creatively overcome. A lot of what we deem to be a hindrance is just an excuse for not moving forward. In this chapter, I'll outline the challenges we, as single parents, face and ways to overcome these challenges.

All the Responsibility

When you initially become a lone parent, it feels quite daunting. Tasks and chores that you had previously divided up with your ex-partner, are now your sole responsibility. You may be shouldering all the childcare, and holding down a job plus running a home. It's a lot, there is no denying it. You must stop thinking of yourself as alone and ask for help. Think who can be of assistance and ask willing family members, grandparents, aunts and uncles, to help with childcare. The father too should help, if he is still in the picture, so that you get some time to yourself. If you need odd jobs done at home, maybe ask a capable friend or find yourself a local handyman. If your children are old enough, they can contribute to household chores, or if you can, hire a cleaner for a couple of hours a week. It is amazing walking into your home when someone else has been in and cleaned, even if it's a rare occurrence.

Tiredness

Fatigue is a common trait, especially for those with young children who don't yet sleep through the night. It is an active life being a single parent and often, as soon as you sit down to relax a little voice pipes up and pulls you to your feet once again. Stress is a big energy eater, so look at your stress levels and work towards stress liberation. Doing regular exercise will give you added energy and help with the stress. To begin with it will feel like the last thing that you want to do, yet even if you only sit on an exercise bike for 20 minutes every other day, or walk to school, over time the exercise effort will pay off and you will appreciate the good feeling that it gives you.

Make sure you get yourself into a regular sleep pattern and if you are having problems sleeping consult a health professional. Make time in your evening to relax before you go to bed, put the worries aside and change your perspective. Meditation is a great way to relax and let go, or listen to calming music whilst taking a bath. Find your way to quieten your mind and relax your body, so that you are ready to sleep.

Eating the right diet is paramount to your feeling of wellbeing. Often our diets can drain us of our energy – drinking caffeine-loaded coffees is not the answer to energy. If you can, organise sleepovers for your children with a willing relative once or twice a month - if not more so that you can have a night off and a much-deserved lie-in. Proper rest and down time is so important. When tiredness strikes, it steals our patience and rationality. Tiredness is not just a symptom of being physically active, it can be caused by mental unrest and emotional unbalances. Try and identify where your tiredness is stemming from – it may be all three. After a good night's sleep, you will have a clear head and renewed energy to deal with any problems or concerns. Once a week, give yourself a permission slip for days off from chores and routine – have an easy day. No one is going to judge you poorly for it and you deserve it.

Financial Pressure

If you don't receive a wedge of **monthly maintenance** making ends meet is challenging, when you are the sole bread winner and chief carer.

There are very few things that decrease in price and childcare is costly. After paying for the essentials – home, heating, water, taxes, food, travel, fuel – it doesn't always leave you enough for much else.

It can be common for a solo parent to end up in debt, just from trying to make ends meet and provide for their children. You can end up stuck in the credit game of increasing interest rates and just affording to cover the monthly repayments. This is a much-generalised statement and of course doesn't apply to all single parents. If you are in debt speak to an unbiased professional (Citizens Advice for example) who can offer you impartial advice on how to deal with it. Don't sit on debt as it only grows and in the process causes you a lot of worry and sleepless nights.

Living on a budget is an answer and reducing cost where you can. Join discount websites, which give you offers on travel, activity outings etc. Annually check price comparison websites, to make sure that you are on the most competitive rates. Speak to Citizens Advice and your local government office about additional benefits that maybe available to you, for example housing support and tax credits.

If you have hit rock bottom financially, visit local food bank charities. Charitable organisations like food banks are staffed by volunteers. They are not there to judge you, they are there to help you and your family get back on your feet. Please never be embarrassed to ask for help, it is exactly what it has been set up for. Life sometimes throws us all curve balls. It doesn't mean that you will be in this situation forever.

For those with children who are under 16-years-old, or under 20 and in full time education, you are entitled to receive child maintenance if you are the main carer day-to-day. In the UK, the government has set up the Child Support Agency (CSA) or the Child Maintenance service, to be found at gov.uk. These organisations are known as 'statutory child maintenance services'. They work out how much you should be paid – they can also collect the payments for you. These organisations can help find the other parent, if you don't know where they live, sort out any disagreements about parentage, work out how much maintenance you should be paid, arrange for the paying parent to pay the child support, pass the payments onto the receiving parent and review changes of circumstance. They can also act if payments are not made.

Time Management

Being a parent is an active life – being a lone parent is extra-active. I feel as though I am rushing from A to B all day long. From the school drop off, to work, back to school, to the activities, then to get dinner on the table, the laundry, the list to do's is often ongoing – and I imagine that your life is no different.

Firstly, give yourself enough time so that you are not rushing. Change the way you think about time. Forget the rushing thoughts, instead focus your on having enough time to get everything that is needed to be done. Prioritise your 'to do' list. When you make the time you have work for you, your stress levels will go down. Write a timetable for you and the children, so you know where you are from day to day. Be sure to schedule yourself in for a bit of relaxing time. And schedule family fun in too, amongst the chores, drop-offs and pick-ups. Time is a valuable commodity, so try to use it as wisely as possible.

Loneliness and Isolation

It is very easy to spend every night at home. There always seems something to do and babysitters are an added expense to what can already be a tight budget. Loneliness hit me when I first separated from my husband and my daughter was still small. I felt lonely, the house was so quiet, there was no one there to share my daily tales with (my daughter wasn't speaking at that stage), meaning there were no spoken interactions. I felt trapped in a lonely world where picking up the phone and having a good natter to friends made all the difference.

Feeling lonely and isolated are also symptoms of depression, a general feeling of feeling detached from society. Talk to a professional to help you reclaim your confidence and joie de vie, if needed, so that you feel that you can socialise again and meet new people. You will feel so much better for going out and interacting with people, so don't hide away as it only perpetuates the feeling. When you feel happy, loneliness has no hold over you. I spend many nights home alone, but I am quite happy with my own company. I have plenty to do, a voice is always at the other end of a phone and social days can be arranged in a heartbeat.

Ask a relative or friend to mind your children. Often they will help if they can, because they want to see you living your life. Loved ones don't want to see you stuck in a flat or house by yourself night after night – they want you to have a life beyond the four walls. I spend time with friends whom have children of similar ages to my daughter and we go on outings, have barbecue evenings together, we hang out and have chatty, fun times. If you focus on family fun gatherings, you don't need to worry about babysitters. Join clubs, classes connect with other parents, find new friends with common interest, the world is filled with some pretty awesome people who have future friend potential. Other solutions to combat loneliness are moving into a house share or taking up residence in a community-focused environment. These are becoming increasingly popular. There are also single-parent charitable organisations, which offer local support in your area, where you can meet up with other single parents. There are organised single-parent holidays that you can go on too, which are geared up to cater for single parents and their families in a supportive setting.

Socialising

Certainly as a single parent, with sole or partial responsibility for your children, having the time to socialise can be a compromise. I have many happily married friends who can pop out at the drop of a hat and meet up with each other. For me, it takes more planning. There isn't the same amount of freedom to enjoy spontaneous nights. These are temporarily on hold until the children are able and trustworthy enough to stay home alone. When everyone is seemingly out and about and you are home alone, it can really affirm your singleness. There are other times when you are excluded from couple's nights out, which are tactless reminders that you are no longer in the 'happily married' gang. It hurts, yet it can happen and if this is the case and your singleness unbalances the 'couple gang' status quo, it is time to make new, additional friendships. Meet up with other single parents or singletons, whom are on the same social vibe as you. It's important for your wellbeing to have some fun too.

Feeling Overwhelmed

Feeling overwhelmed by life can quite often stop you in your tracks. It's as if you have arrived at a crossroads and have no idea which way to turn for the best result. When you feel like this, take some time before making big decisions, talk things through with friends and trusted advisers. Detach from the things that are making you feel overwhelmed by taking some time out. Temporarily put the problems in an imaginary box and mentally let go, until a solution presents itself that you feel comfortable with. If you are feeling overwhelmed by the responsibility, ask for help. When you open up and share with others how you are feeling, you are allowing them to assist you, even if they just listen to you. Often a good night's sleep gives you a fresh perspective on life. A long walk in nature can be very healing, or maybe just leave the house for a couple of days with your children and go and have some quality fun time – these things should certainly help. If they don't and you are in a deeper state of despair, then seek professional help. Whether that's from an allopathic doctor or a holistic therapist, the sheer fact that you are facing your feelings is a step in the right direction.

The 'I can't' Feeling

Start by believing that you can, because when you put your mind to something, everything can become possible. Be aware of your mental chatter – observe your thoughts and what you tell yourself. If you are always having self-deprecating thoughts about yourself and your life situation, you won't be able to move forward with ease and you can get stuck in a rut. If you talk to yourself positively and respectfully, you will be amazed at the changes it can create. It's all about flicking the 'on' switch to "I can".

"I can't" is just an excuse. Take some time to work out what is the real issues behind the excuses that are keeping you from "I can". Is it worry, not trusting in the flow of life, not wanting more happiness for yourself, fear? Let your inner wisdom in your heart guide you. We should sometimes take risks in life that push us past our comfort zone, to reap greater happiness.

Guilt

Guilt got me! I felt guilty for being a failure as a wife, as a mother and as me. A lot of my destructive thoughts came as a result of the constant abusive putdowns by my ex-husband, I started to believe his cruelness. I felt guilt that I hadn't been able to keep the family unit together, for the sake of my daughter. I was sending my daughter's father away from her. I felt guilt towards my ex-husband for separating him from his daughter, who he really cherished. My thoughts were unrealistic and very illogical. If I had stayed with my husband, the reign of terror that I lived in would probably have escalated, leading to possible fatal consequences. Yet that guilt was forever present. I took on the sole responsibility for the failure of the marriage and yet in reality I had tried everything I could to help my husband. He wasn't willing and he blamed me for being me. If you feel guilt towards yourself for being you, then let it go, for those thoughts do not serve you. You are more than enough – start loving what you are.

As I started to emerge from the fog, I began to see more clearly and saw that I wasn't solely to blame. I had done the right thing for myself and my daughter. No child deserves to grow up in a house of warring parents. They should be protected from such – so that they don't believe this to be the normal way to behave. It is also frightening for children and hugely sad for them to see their parents in volatile situations. Home is meant to be safe, loving and nurturing place where you can all flourish. Feeling guilt is an emotion that doesn't serve anything. Self-forgiveness banishes feelings of guilt. Begin to forgive yourself and let go of any judgement that you may be holding onto.

Addiction

Having an addiction is a form of escapism. Being a single parent can be filled with many challenges, and rather than face them, it can be easier to escape them. Addictions usually stem from doing something that makes us feel temporarily happy. From our chosen 'happy buzz addiction' we find some relief from what we are feeling inside.

It could be an addiction to eating, drinking, love or the search for love, shopping or substance abuse. A harmless habit can become something that you engage in compulsively. If your addiction is out of control, seek professional help. There are helplines, with trained advisers, who can guide you to take positive steps to break the addiction. There are many 'anonymous' groups, catering for a wide range of addictions, from alcoholism to sex. They offer the '12 steps to recovery' programmes. You will also find them to be very supportive and non-judgemental. They will be able to give you the tools you need to break the pattern. Addictions can happen. Whether you are suffering with an addiction that is causing you harm or not, then it is time to change. Addictions hold us hostage, so we can no longer participate freely in our life. Don't judge yourself harshly, things happen and sometimes other things help us to escape those things that have happened. Take the right steps to break the cycle, by talking to someone, or joining a suitable support group.

If your relationship has just ended because of your partner has been suffering with addiction, get yourself some support. Being in a co-dependant relationship can be very draining. Al-Anon Nar-Anon or Gam-Anon (to name a few) are support groups set up to help and support families of addicts. It can be a real help to speak with other people who have experienced what you have and see how they dealt with it. It can be very stressful being in a relationship with an addict, as their choices effect your whole families lives and living in that uncertainty is very draining until enough is enough.

Fear of the Future

When you marry, or you are in a lasting, long-term relationship, there is a degree of security. If one of you in that partnership gets sick, loses a job, wants to retrain, you can usually work a way out, whereby one can support the other. Having two combined incomes helps financially and enables you to save for the future. When you are alone, that person and what their presence represented is no longer there. Their support, the safety net of the partnership has vanished. And with that often brings about feelings of terrible inner loneliness and a fear of how the future will turn out. It is stressful being the sole provider for your future. And it would be only natural to wonder, how long you can keep juggling to make ends meet and if it was ever going to become easier?

This can result in being overly-cautious and not living your life to its full potential. Just for the record, we all have a lot of potential in our lives to fulfil. It is important to remember that we don't know what any of our futures hold in store for us. What we do know is that we can take positive steps in the present, so that our future can be more prosperous. Our children aren't children forever. When they are well into their teens, they don't need you to be around as much as they did when they were small. Take advantage of this new phase. Become more ambitious at work, put yourself up for the promotions, the bigger salaries. Do what you need to do, so that you are giving yourself the best opportunity to succeed. If your children are still quite small, speak to your employer about pension plans. In the UK since 2013, all businesses should be offering employees to pay into a pension plan. Open a savings account. Whatever you put away is something towards your 'pot'. On your quiet nights in, learn more and expand your horizons.

To Single Fathers Out There, Everywhere

I salute, respect and honour you. I, as many single mums out there, had a child with a man who simply didn't know how to be a father. He was unable to step up to the challenge and take the responsibility to be a dad. I look at single dads with so much admiration. You are an amazing example of a man and a father.

I know that the single parent statistics are a bit 'mum' heavy and because of this, single fathers and their situation often get overlooked or excluded. Certainly, the majority of support is aimed at the mother market. I am not sure how it would make me feel if the shoe was on the other foot. I probably would feel excluded, invisible and isolated. Your main struggles, your daily struggles, are no different to those faced by a single mother. But there does seem to be a lack of support and understanding. Our society has for many years dictated that men should be out there hunting and gathering, whilst the women stay home and attend to the womanly duties. Being a single dad means that you are doing both and it can feel like you are terribly out of your depth until you find a sure footing. It may be that you are unable to carry on working, for example if you need to be with the children all day long and to attend to their needs. It's hard adjusting. And it takes strength and courage to step up and do what you are doing.

Many preschool children groups are geared towards mothers and it must often feel awkward trying to fit in. I imagine that women often sound as though we are speaking in a totally different language. What is amazing is your willingness to try, to going to unfamiliar and not necessarily comfortable situations for your children.

I know that you to have suffered the heartbreak of losing the mother of your child, as well as your partner. As with many single mothers, when you found out that you were going to be a parent, you had no idea that you would be the one raising your children alone. It is hard to understand why the mother who carried your child is unable to mother her children, handing over the totality of the parenting responsibility to you. You must know what an amazing thing you are doing – you are selflessly loving your child and holding together your family unit. It's huge. And you should congratulate yourself.

From my perspective, I carried my daughter and birthed her. I couldn't imagine not wanting to be the mother to my daughter, or to be her main carer. I can see compassionately and without judgement that some women are unable to mother. Whether it's for reasons of mental unbalance, career preference choice, the desire for freedom – I can understand that. Parenting isn't an easy task. Some women find it almost impossible to bond with their child and the pain and sense of failure can be too overwhelming to feel, so then it's easier to walk away and try to forget. Like abandoning fathers, there are those mothers who don't want the responsibility and abscond from their children's lives. It happens and it's happening.

It is an attractive quality in a man, to see him bond and love his children. To take responsibility of their wellbeing. You may not necessarily feel attractive, when you have been spread so thinly with the day-to-day of being a single parent. However, the ability to love and be responsible for another is a very appealing trait, and silently it speaks volumes.

With the increasing numbers of single dads, there have been some support groups set up especially for you. They have often been set up by single fathers and they offer advice, support, life coaching and kindness. If you feel in any doubt about how you are coping, it is wise to seek help. Who better to get advice from than a brother that has walked the very same path that you are.

As much as friends can offer you support and their loyalty, they may not understand and be able to empathise with your situation and the demands upon your time. Being a married father, isn't the same as having total responsibility. With your close friends, explain to them what you are going through and how you feel, so that they may begin to understand. They no doubt will respect you and all that you are doing.

Much of the practical advice I can offer to you is the same as I would suggest for single mothers. It is important to you find your inner happy barometer, for your children, but for you too. Don't feel isolated and alone, because you are not. Ask for help if you feel that you are struggling. If you are suddenly entering a world domestic vulnerability, ask for some guidance – from a friend, a sister or your mum – to give you a few pointers in the right direction. Having a few 'pull it out the bag' recipes and a few housewifery tricks can really help you settle into your all-encompassing role and give you confidence.

We live in a time where things are changing constantly. The old image of men being solely the hunter and gather is fading and outmoded. Don't feel emasculated if you are having to spend more time than you would like to cleaning the bathtub, or running around with a vacuum cleaner. Think of it as empowering, because you are smashing the old male stereotypes. You are representing the new man, a man who is stepping up and taking on the world of family. Being a parent is a huge blessing. Of course, it's not going to smell of roses 100% of the time, but the unity and bonds that you and your children are creating are priceless and they will surpass and supersede most things that life has to offer. Enjoy it, for life is short.

CHAPTER 6

Managing The Day - Today

L ife goes by so quickly. Some days are busy from the moment you wake until the time your head hits the pillow. Organising school projects, house chores, laundry, preparing meals, assisting with homework, catching up on work, holding down a job – the lists can sometimes feel endless.

The key to helping your day to flow with grace, and to have quality time with your children and yourself, is of course time management. Time management is all about being super organised and on the case. A calm mind, so that you have mental clarity, helps too. Multitasking and prioritising your daily jobs helps.

I find that giving myself a day off, a chore-less day is very refreshing and is much needed. You will know what you can get away with doing and not doing. No one is going to judge you if you haven't whipped round the house with a duster for a day or three. Invest in a dishwasher, it saves so much time. You can get a cleaner to give you regular help, or to help with big seasonal cleans, to take the pressure off you. Get your laundry done in a service wash if you are fed up of your home looking like a Chinese laundry service. As much as organisation plays a part, so does being creative with your time management.

Eventually everything that you need to do will get done.

- Get a diary or wall calendar, write down every commitment, every appointment, school activity, birthday etc that comes your way, so things don't get forgotten

- Create a routine that works for you all, so that you have quality family time together. Draw up the family timetable and put it up on the wall
- Create a weekly meal plan that is sympathetic to your available time
- Home delivery and weekly grocery shops - online shopping is great if you are unable to physically get to the shops
- Lay out clothes and get PE kits and activity clothes ready the night before
- Stay on top of the domestic chores and home maintenance
- Get rid of outgrown clothes (charity, jumble, recycling), avoid hoarding, declutter regularly
- Know where things are in your home, file paperwork, organise seasonal outdoor wear etc
- Write achievable 'to do' lists that fit in with your day or week
- Set up standing orders and direct debits for bills and other outgoings
- Write a weekly/monthly budget so you know where you are financially
- Programme reminders into your computer or smart phone diary, so that you know where you are with things like dental, medical and optical check-ups, term dates, car MOTs and tax returns
- Schedule special time for you and your children into your day.

Financial Flow

Money makes the world go around, the world go around, the world go around! Actually, it is LOVE that makes the world go around – we just need money to live the life that we would like to live. Money is a great asset, as it opens the door to many opportunities. Money is something that everyone living in this modern consumer-based society needs to survive. Little seems to be free in the world presently and costs for our basic needs seem to be ever-increasing.

As a single parent, it is often difficult to balance raising your children and working, yet it is possible and it becomes more possible when you can recognise your strengths as well as your limitations. Not all single parents need to work – some choose not to, some are supported by the child/children's father – although there is an increasing number that do work out of necessity. In many cases there is a need for both parents to work, even if you are still in a partnership. Mothers are having to return to work much sooner, when the children are still small, to help make the money ends meet.

Divorce, Maintenance and Having to Return to Earning

With most divorce cases, there is a financial agreement drawn up, which is agreed legally during the divorce hearing. Financial agreements are unique to the separating couple, so there is no good in making comparisons between your settlement and someone else's. Due to the change of the martial circumstances, it is often the case that you may have had to return to work to supplement the monthly maintenance contribution. It can of course be quite overwhelming, putting yourself back into the employment arena after years of being a stay-at-home mum.

Handy tips for getting back in the work place

- Refresh your work skills by doing an evening course. Investigate to see how your job has evolved since your employment
- Retrain and get new qualifications. There are so many flexible courses on offer that you can do from home, in your own time
- Draw from the skills that you have experienced as a mother. Multi-tasking, being responsible, team management, time management, PA skills, compassionate and nurturing nature. All these are wonderful assets to any business or workplace environment
- Be confident. Walk into job interviews with a healthy glow of confidence and knowing that you can rock the job
- Remember to sell yourself. Present yourself well for job interviews and practice interviewing techniques with friends.

Feel prepared and acknowledge all your skills and what you have done previously

- Write a realistic list to yourself outlining your ideal salary, hours, commute time, annual leave etc that would suit you for now, so that you are approaching the right jobs
- Remember that as your life's demands change, so too can your work. So, look for a job where promotion is possible, or a job that can offer you additional training.

When I separated from my husband, I was already in employment and I earned a reasonable salary. Not life-changing, but enough to get by on. I wasn't in a job that necessarily ignited my heart with passion nor did it fulfil my life's dream. Yet it served its purpose and I was surrounded by good people, whom offered friendship and familiarity. My daily commute was long. It was a busy job, which came with responsibilities, but it too came with many positive attributes. I was able to drop my daughter to school, and be home by 6.00pm to start our evening rituals. I also had a good relationship with my employer, which I really valued. This had been cultivated over the many years that I had worked for him. He knew that I was a single parent and was sympathetic to me taking my annual leave during the school holidays.

It is always important to focus upon the positives that a job will give you, rather than fixating on the negatives, otherwise you'll send yourself crazy. Accepting your current employment for what it is, is a good way to find happy, if it means that you can spend more time with your children. When your children are small they really need their mum to be around and to be present with them. I personally would hold off on the high-earning, high power jobs, when the children are very small, unless you have an amazing support and back-up team – both in the work place and at home. And when you walk through the door marked home, you can totally detach from the workplace, so that you can spend quality time with your children. Life flows with ease when there is balance in place.

Many employers now offer flexible working times, job shares and opportunities to work from home. It's worth you having a meeting with your employer and discussing what would suit you both. I changed my working week to four days instead of five. I still did the same amount of work, but it was squeezed into four days. It meant I had one day where I didn't have to face a long commute and I was able to collect my daughter at the end of her school day, which delighted her and me. The change to my working week made all the difference to my mental state.

State Benefits

Living on benefits isn't easy and it can be challenging to make ends meet. It can be okay in the short-term, yet it isn't really a long-term solution. You may choose to stay at home with your children and benefits may enable you to do this. If you have plans to return to work, you may be able to retrain during this time. The government is always keen to see people returning to work and there are discounted courses available, so that you may polish up on skills and learn new ones. You can find details about this out at your local employment office. State benefits available include unemployment benefit, rent allowance and child support. Working Tax Credits and Child Tax Credits help to top up a low income and they also help towards child care. It is best to discuss what benefits are available to you with Citizens Advice or with a government adviser, as the benefit system is forever changing.

Your Own Business

When your children are more self-sufficient and you feel that you can balance home and work, then it is probably the right time to follow your dream career path, if you have one, and move forward to create the career reality that you desire. It is important to be happy within your working life, because it takes up a lot of your time. And more than likely in this modern-day climate you will be working long after your children leave home. There are plenty of successful single mums and dads. Some of whom have created small start-up businesses that have rolled into huge successes. Often a business idea is created though a 'need', a gap in the market. Pay attention to the ideas that pop into your mind. These could have the potential to become financial goldmines. Success is often measured in financial gain. To be truly successful is to be happy and passionate, whilst earning money. Really follow your inner passion – maybe you have creative abilities, or you would like to become a councillor, a published author or set up a business providing a service that your feel enthused about. If you are unsure about your ideas talk it over with a 'think box' team, or if you are selling things, try them out locally at product related venues to see the general response and to gauge the levels of interest. You won't know unless you try. If your business comprehension needs fine tuning, invest some time into doing a business course, to learn how to create a viable business plan, to balance to books and generate the all-important profit.

There are many ways to work at home. You could prepare food for a farmers' market, if baking or food production is your thing. If your skills lend themselves to these careers, you could try graphic design, telesales, accounting, being a virtual assistant, translator, tutoring, web development, offer technical support, writer/editor, a medical transcriptionist, hair dressing or selling over the internet – companies like eBay can provide you with a global selling platform. There are now many opportunities available that allow you to stay at home and help you to create your own business.

Utilising your talents as a Single Parent

As a single parent, life teaches you how to be a successful multi-tasker, be an astute planner, to be money savvy, a triumphant time keeper, a selfless carer and a full-time personal assistant. These are all wonderful skills that you bring with you to a job. Single parents can make wonderful employees, as often they are solely responsible for keeping the roof over their family's heads. Don't sell yourself short, you have a lot to bring to a job and would be a very diligent employee. Being a parent helps you to connect to children – you could retrain as teaching assistant or teacher, which would give you similar hours and holidays to your children. It's not just teaching jobs available within the educational system, there are other roles such as accounting, catering or nursing too.

Creating Abundance and Prosperity

What is abundance, what is prosperity? To create, you firstly need to understand what true abundance is and what real prosperity means. It's not just financial gain or reward, it's about so much more. It's about being truly, deeply happy, it's about being filled with vitality, good health and enthusiasm for life. It's about being peacefully contented and graciously grateful for all that you presently have and for all that you want to create in your life. It's about being generous. Abundance and prosperity are the celebration of life. It's about living the life that any Godly parent would wish for their child.

How do you want your daughter or son's life to pan out? You of course want to see them glowing with optimum health. You want to see them happy and peaceful. You want to see them courageously chasing the dreams that are held within their being. You would see them financially secure, living in a safe and comfortable home. They would be generous and kind to those around them and help strangers in need. They would be loved and supported by friends and they would be in a deep and tender loving relationship. They would have it all. They would be truly abundant and they would prosper in every aspect of their lives.

So now let's return to you and your creating all that you wish for you and your children. Creating something new begins with the idea of what you would like to attract into your life. Whether it is more money, improved health, a safe dwelling, a new love. You need to focus positively upon it and take steps to make the changes in your life that will help you create your new reality. When you are on track you will be amazed at what suddenly shows up. New people, opportunities, lucky breaks. Don't focus on what you don't want, otherwise you will attract more of the same.

This is known as the universal law of attraction. For example, if you put your mental energy onto your mounting debt, guess what? More debt will come, because that is what you are thinking about. I can hold my hand up to this. So, you must change where you are putting your mental energy, your mental energy is creating your reality. Instead of focusing on debt, open a savings account and deposit £20 per week, per month, whatever you can. But know that you are saving and you have money, it's the opposite of thinking of debt. Of course, take responsibility for your debt, but let it go mentally.

For an alternative example, have you ever woken up in the morning, bumped your head and grumpiness has set in? This grumpy mind-set created a catalogue of mishaps that filled your day. Depending on how we react to something can determine what comes our way in the future. Thoughts and feelings create our reality, so keep them on the path that you wish to walk down. Focus on the positives within yourself and others, within your life, your neighbourhood. You can do this by writing an appreciation or gratitude list. The more that we focus on the good, the more of it we will see. It's a wonderful way to heal relationships, just by focusing on the positive aspects of a person. That includes the relationship with yourself.

Abundance Meditation

This mediation was given to me by one of my spiritual teachers. I found that it has worked for me to see where I was at in my 'universal financial flow'. Abundance is an energy and as with all energies, it can change.

- Sit quietly and mentally observe your breathing to quieten your mind
- Imagine that you are standing at a riverbank looking at the river. The river is flowing into the ocean of abundance. In this ocean is everything that you could possibly need
- Keep breathing and visualising this river. Now imagine that a physical representation, a being of prosperity comes to stand next to you and asks you to jump into the river
- Note your reaction. How does it make you feel? Do you feel unworthy to receive, do you feel fearful, do you feel that you don't deserve to jump into the abundant flow? If you jump, how is the water – is it still, is it fast flowing?
- Your reaction will be your inner barometer, to show you what you are willing to receive. It is our held-onto beliefs about our

self-worth, how much we value ourselves, or you may have inherited negative ideas surrounding money, which stops you from receiving

- Still sitting in the meditation, ask the being of prosperity to help assist you in changing your thought patterns, so that they are in alignment to receive gratefully
- Keep practising this meditation until you see yourself excitedly and trustingly jumping into a fast-flowing river that is going to take you to the ocean of abundance. Once you are in the ocean, float and trust that everything you need will come.

You can also use EFT – Emotional Freedom Techniques – NLP – Neuro Linguistic Programming and affirmations to help to shift your consciousness from a place of lack, to being ready to receive all that you desire.

Visualise what you want to attract to your life, as if it has already happened. Feel the emotions of the joy you will feel when you get the job you want, the soul-mate relationship and a clean bill of health. Everyday put some of your energy into creating the life that you wish. Create a vision board, an aspiration list, a request letter to the universe. Look at it daily and really imagine it manifesting in the most joyous and beautiful way. One of the keys to successful visualisation is to be incredibly happy and grateful and see to yourself in your new car, or your new job, or being blissfully loved up in a kind and respectful relationship, or to see yourself full of confidence.

Take appropriate steps to help you go in the direction that you want to be going. If it's a slimmed down and toned physique you are after, then take the steps you need to make that happen. Change your diet and do a little work out – even 10 minutes a day is going to make you feel that you are going in the right direction. Visualise yourself with the body that you want. Ask, be patient, trust, take positive steps towards your goals. At the right time and when you are ready, the right opportunity, person, bit of luck or idea, will show up. You must follow your inner nudges and intuitive feelings, so that you are in that right place at the right time, to get you to the life that you know is waiting for you.

CHAPTER 7

Finding The Joy In Being A Lone Parent

Y ou get one life, this one, so why would you not want to live it with joy? You cannot change what has happened in the past. But you can learn from the events that took place along your journey to the present moment. The present is now and it's the time you have with your children that matters. Creating fantastic memories together so that you remember the life and times that you had together with joy in your hearts. Before you know it, they will forge their own lives in this world and kissing a bump better no longer holds the magic cure. Don't waste too much time in grieving for the life you think you had or wanted. Find the joy in this phase. When we are joyful and accepting, we attract more joyful things into our lives. Maybe that is experiences, new people, fun times, new loves.

Our children are such gifts, they help us remember the simplicity of life, if you allow them to teach you. They have no judgement. When they are small their innocence is so refreshing, their honesty is often priceless. I bet you can all remember moments as a parent when your child has been so honest that you wished the floor would swallow you up, but what they said has been undeniably truthful. Motherhood, fatherhood is simply great. No child is a perfect angel and no child will never press your buttons. That's their job, to help you master qualities such as patience, compassion, kindness, serenity. On a practical parenting level, they teach you discipline, by the seemingly constantly-enforced boundaries. As a lone parent, it's not so easy when there is no back up, yet this can help you to stand up for the things that you believe in with courage.

I found that my daughter has helped me to know myself. I know my limits because she has found many of them. Because of the unsurpassed love I have for her and my willingness to not react unfavourably, I have learnt to stay centred and at peace and not to react like a crazy wound up toy.

Being a lone parent is challenging on some levels, there is no denying that. Yet you have the opportunity to form very close bonds with your children because it's 'just you guys'. I talk to my daughter and let her know what's going on with me honestly, all the time, we understand each other. When your child is older, with their own children, they will understand the loving sacrifices that you made for them. They will remember how hard you worked to keep the family together and a roof over their heads. You will have shaped these beautiful beings in less than easy circumstances and it's your strength of character and the love you have for your child that has helped them to be grounded, well-balanced individuals later in life.

There was a time when I wasn't feeling a great deal of joy about being a lone parent. I was wallowing in self-pity and was stuck in a negative state of mind. And that was fine, I needed to lick my wounds. But in the long term it wasn't healthy and so I changed my perspective of the way that I looked at things. Instead of looking down, I started to look up.

There were times along my own journey that I felt as though I was wearing stilettos whilst climbing up a foggy, ice covered mountain. Whilst climbing up that mountain, the ice began to melt and I was given mountaineering boots and it became easier. I could stand up straight and observe, and I could see the joy all around me and the joy in me. Not having a husband hadn't made me a failure, nor did it stop my daughter from living a jubilant life. I felt an incredible freedom. I no longer had the stress that came with and from my husband. There was this wonderful freedom of not having to keep trying to make a triangular marriage fit into a round box of contentment. I could raise my daughter how I chose, without the constant look of judgement and criticism. I was no longer living in fear, I was totally free. And it's that freedom that lets me and my daughter jump in the car at 6 am and go on little adventures to unexplored lands. It's the same freedom that allows us to stay in pyjamas until 2 pm whilst constructing Lego palaces and eating homemade muffins. The life I live with my daughter is priceless and I am grateful to all those who have held my hand on this journey. We are never truly alone.

To find the joy you first must give yourself permission to feel it. Down tools, ignore the 'to do' list and have some time out. You deserve it. There is so much pressure on parents, coming from so many different angles and there are pressures 24/7 in being a lone parent. Whether you need time out with your children or without, that's fine because no one's judging you. It so important for your overall wellbeing to regain that joyful feeling and not have to be responsible. Responsibility can sometimes take over. Don't allow it to become a burden, keep the balance. Laugh – laughter is one of the best forms of free therapy available to us. When you laugh, you get blasted by the feel-good hormones.

Support in Raising your Child

One of the challenges that I faced was feeling alone and unsupported. My daughter's father wasn't present and so all the choices regarding her upbringing fell at my feet and the raising of my daughter was ultimately my responsibility. However, I didn't live on a desert island in the middle of a vast ocean, so I wasn't alone at all. Rather than share concerns or debating choices with my daughter's father (who was no longer communicating with me) about what is the best way to raise our child, I formed a supportive circle around me. This was made up of family members and close friends, who had both mine and especially my daughter's best interests at heart. The final decisions were always mine. However, the support was there to sound out concerns and provide advice, which helped me reach good and balanced solutions.

As well as offering advice, they also offer childcare which I am truly grateful for. My daughter loves spending time with her family, as they do with her. And when she is in their presence, I know that she is safe and happy, which gives me huge peace of mind. It is important to set boundaries regarding childcare. That way people do what they feel happy doing and it's done with pleasure, rather than a burden. I try my best to respect others' lives and feelings, so that if they can't help, I don't take it personally. Everyone has the choice to do what is best for them and this includes you too. If you are a working parent, having a childminder or an after-school club organised are good solutions to childcare. I wouldn't feel happy or relaxed expecting my friends to constantly help – it can really tarnish your relationship, for obvious reason. Children feel safe with routine. My parents collect my daughter from school twice a week and then she either goes to after-school club or a childminder. She knows what's going on in her life. If needed there is financial support out there, to assist you with childcare.

If your child's father is still present in their life, they too can shoulder the responsibility in the happy upbringing of your child/children, by offering financial support, joint decision-making and regular and supportive childcare. When you have moved past the hurt and pain of the separation it becomes easier to work as a team, especially when you both start viewing each other with respect and honouring one another as your child's parents. This harmony has such a positive effect on your child or children. If they see that their parents are stood united in bring them up it help to keep a cocoon of love and security around them. No one likes to be the cause of arguments especially children.

As your children become older, their need for you becomes less. The parental attachment is of course still there, but they should confidence to stay with friends for sleepovers or enjoy lone play days. It's a great way to carve some 'you time' into your day. And when you repay the sleepover and play date, you are giving the gift of space back to the other parent in return. It's a win-win situation!

You also need some external support for yourself. If you have a good group of friends that are compassionate towards you, then that is wonderful. It is also an idea to find a local single parent support group. It is good to connect with those who understand how you feel, who have been in your situation, who have moved on gracefully and can offer advice and compassion. I love my happily married friends, and I enjoy their company. However, there are some things that they cannot relate too.

Help

Asking for help – be it financial, childcare or help in assembling a chest of drawers from a flat pack – used to make me feel like a failed woman. I am not sure why. Probably it was my independent ego. I was bought up in a generation where women were meant to be multi-tasking superheroes, with the world at their feet. And asking for help wasn't really on my agenda. I really liked being independent, it gave me a sense of freedom and inner strength. So, having to start to ask for help initially made me feel weak and uncomfortable and very vulnerable, just in case I was told to take a hike.

However, asking for help is not a weakness at all. It's brave to know and accept your limitation. It may be that not everyone can help you, as they aren't able to. But they may be able to point you in the direction of someone who can. Asking for help gives someone else the joy and opportunity to do something for you, which they may feel happy about. Feeling useful and appreciated is a great feeling.

There are amazing charities and organisations which can help you with financial advice, counselling, career direction and benefit support, lists of which can be found in the back of this book. My advice to you is choose your help wisely – speak with those who have experience and can advise authentically. Don't go to a serial bigamist for marital advice, to a crook for financial advice, or to someone who is obviously malnourished for nutrition advice. The best people are those who have faced adversity and have overcome it and have learnt a great deal of sense on their journey.

I was left in a huge financial dilemma. I felt that I couldn't burden my family with it, as they on some level would feel responsible for sorting it out. The debt certainly wasn't their fault and I didn't feel comfortable in sharing, as I knew they would worry if they didn't help me. In hindsight would I, should I, have shared my problems with them? Who knows, although I very much doubt it? I did panic initially. I feared bailiffs looting my home, of my flat being repossessed. I was living in worst-case scenario mode and couldn't see the wood for the trees. Much of the debt I had acquired was a parting gift from my ex-husband, a gift that just kept growing. I did finally find help with a debt management solution. Some companies are more authentic than others and avoid those who promise the world, then require a lot of fees in return. I would advise seeking independent advice before signing and committing to anything. I also sought counselling as a way of helping to make sense of the experience of being in a domestically abusive relationship. I knew that it would really hurt and deeply upset my loved ones if I offloaded the dark side to my marriage in graphic detail to them, for the obvious reason: they love me.

Of course, I ask my family and friends for other kinds of help, childcare, advice, emergency relief, DIY skills, love advice etc. When you need help ask for it, it's a sign of inner strength. Try not to be attached to the outcome. Helping someone out is an act of giving kindness and that feels good.

Gratitude

Being in a mind-set of gratitude really helps you to feel supported and loved. I know it sounds like a cliché, but when you start to see the little generosities that are given to you, it helps you to feel great about yourself. They can be as small as someone saying, "Wow your hair looks great today". Gratitude journals have become popular, since the hit film 'The Secret' – a film about manifesting your dreams. Every day you write down the things that you are grateful for. This can include received kind words, material gifts, friends, family and strangers' actions, lessons learnt, hearing an uplifting story, witnessing a divine sunrise or sunset or cloud formation, the dawn of a new day, the roof over your head, the food on your plate, and your kids of course. Just be grateful. And be grateful for being YOU too. Write them all down. By doing so, it just gives you something positive to focus your mind on, rather than what can often feel like a constant flow of worrying thoughts.

Writing in your journal can be a reflective part of your evening routine, whereby you become a witness to your daily life. Even if you didn't feel that you had a great day, understand why – did you not give yourself enough nourishment, you had self-destructive thoughts about the size of your rear end, or someone didn't do the right thing by you?

Whatever the daily drama, a new dawn brings a new day, and with it the opportunity to give yourself time for you, a new perspective on the size of your butt and understand that often others have bad days too – it's not personal. Gratitude helps you not to morph into a grumpy, ungrateful old mare. Being gracious helps to give you a happy footing in your life.

CHAPTER 8

Stress And Getting Back To The 'H' Factor

The H Factor – or Happiness – is important in everyone's lives. There are days when one thing after another goes pear-shaped, you have lost you happy footing and all you want to do is return to a sleepy slumber of comfort, which isn't always possible. Our modern lives are filled with stress and no more so than for a single parent, who has work commitments, sole responsibility for the upbringing of a child, combining this with the common 21st century daily stresses that we all meet. It is important to learn ways to combat stress. This is simply done by recognising the feeling of stress as it rises within you and to then taking appropriate action. Please note that if you suffer from long-term or chronic stress then you should seek professional help, be that a health practitioner or an alternative therapist. It needs to be addressed, as it can have an adverse effect on your present and future health.

A couple of years into my journey as a single parent I crashed. The years of sleep deprivation, money worries, non-stop rushing here to there, work commitments, not having any 'me fun' and just feeling over-burdened by life and responsibility took its toll. I cried uncontrollably, felt like I was living on a razor's edge. I was exhausted and I had no patience to deal with anything, however small, so reacted badly and overdramatised little mishaps. I needed TIME OUT! Up until then I had been quite a chilled-out, optimistic person and stress wasn't something that I had ever suffered with. So it took me a little by surprise. In my case, it was just the build-up of the keep going, happy face-mode. I was shattered and overburdened. The doctor signed me off work for three weeks' bed rest. In those three weeks I sought nutritional advice, homoeopathy consultations, energy healing work and took time to evaluate my life, so that I could make it work with more ease and with a positive flow. At the end of the day stuff happens.

Recognising the symptoms of stress

Stress can manifest itself in many symptoms and when you feel yourself drifting off to the red zone, you can take positive actions so that you may return to the Zen you!

Cognitive Symptoms include:

- Poor memory
- Inability to concentrate
- Poor judgment
- Having a negative mind-set
- A busy and anxious mind
- Worrying thoughts

Emotional Symptoms include:

- Moodiness
- Unable to relax
- Short-fused and irritable
- Feeling overwhelmed, depressed and unhappy
- Feelings of loneliness and isolation

Physical Symptoms include:

- Aches and pains
- Diarrhoea and constipation
- Nausea
- Chest pains, rapid heartbeat
- Shallow breathing

- Loss of sex drive
- Frequent colds and a weak immune system

Behavioural Symptoms Include:

- Eating more or less
- Sleeping too much or too little
- Isolating yourself from others
- Procrastinating or neglecting responsibilities
- Relying on alcohol or other stimulants to relax and escape
- Nervous habits

If any of the above symptoms resonate with you then there are ways of dealing with stress, so don't worry.

Tools to help you deal with Stress

Good, regular sleep patterns

Sleep is our downtime, it's a time when our conscious and unconscious mind process and detach from the waking dramas. It's a chance for our bodies to rejuvenate and regain balance. Sleep is important to our overall wellbeing. If I have worries and concerns before I go to sleep, I often say a prayer to receive guidance and the inner knowing on the best way to deal with them in my waking day. It really works and is a great way to mentally detach from the stressful thoughts.

Taking action

If, for example, it is your work that is causing you to be stressed, identify the problem area and with a friend come up with a reasonable solution that you feel would help relieve some of the stress from you. Then you can speak with your manager, or employer and hopefully come up with a compromise, so that you don't feel so bombarded with work. At the end of the day, we are all much more productive and a pleasure to be around when we are happy.

Accept the things that you cannot change

No one can change everything. Acceptance is a form of surrender, it is what it is for now. Remember nothing really lasts forever, we live in a world of cycles.

Exercise

It is one of the best combatants against stress. Exercising helps to deplete the stress hormones and releases mood-enhancing chemicals that help us to cope with stress. Find an exercise or a couple of different types that you feel happy and confident doing. Exercising a couple of times a week will make you feel like you are on the winning team. Stretch out tense muscles in the yoga studio, pound out frustrations on the squash courts and wash away emotional dramas in the pool.

Volunteering

By helping those who are in a worse situation than you, it really helps to put your problems into perspective. The more that you are able to help or give to the needy, the happier you feel. It's like a wonderful chain-reaction of good karma. And when we feel happy, we feel resilient and less bothered by upsets and problems.

Connect to your friends

Do this for support and fun on a regular basis. Don't sit at home worrying about things, which I do know is easier said than done. If you do have to sit at home, pick up the phone and have a friendly uplifting chat, to distract your mind. Friends are blessings, a problem shared is a problem halved, and they can offer you a fresh outlook.

Have Faith

Surrendering to a power that is greater than you and having a spiritual connection (let's call it 'the love', because surely that is what spirituality truly is), helps to relinquish and let go of the responsibility of the outcome. Trust and know that you will be okay. There are many new age, old age and religious age teachings on how to connect more deeply on a spiritual level.

Take back control

If you can identify the cause of your stress – be it money worries, work overload, domestic pressures – find ways of remedying them. Don't let small problems grow in your mind, until you feel that they are too big for you to deal with. If needed, break it down into manageable steps.

Time management

Prioritise your day. There are things that need to be done and there are things that simply don't need your immediate attention. Learn to be organised so that you don't overwhelm yourself. Write a list of all the things that you need to do in your day.

Tap it out

Tapping is also known as EFT or Emotional Freedom Technique. It is a fantastic tool. Using a specific sequence gently tapping on to meridian points on the body helps to release blockages within the body's energy system. These blockages are often the source of emotional intensities and discomforts. The blocks can lead to limiting beliefs. Resulting symptoms are emotional and physical, including a lack of confidence, self-esteem, anxiety, depression or an addictive behavioural pattern. The technique is a simple yet effective self-help tool, which empowers people to contribute to their own healing and development process. It is super easy and highly effective. A more in-depth discussion of tapping can be found in Chapter 10.

Try to get back to a positive moment.

If you feel a negative or stressful thought pop into your mind, banish it before it can take a hold. Divert your attention to a good memory, to a funny moment, listen to a favourite piece of music.

A Balanced Diet

Eating a balanced and nutritious diet is paramount to our feeling of wellness. If you are suffering from stress, avoid all stimulants: alcohol, caffeine, sugar and highly-processed foods. Enjoy food and drink that boost your immune system. Suffering from stress depletes your immune system.

Talking to a professional listener

Talking to someone can really help to put things in perspective. They can offer non-judgemental advice, as well as a compassionate ear.

Hugging

Long, deep and meaningful hugs help to boost oxytocin, which help to heal feelings of anger, stress and isolation. Hugs also lift serotonin levels, elevating moods and creating happiness. Hugging relaxes muscles and releases tension. Good hugs are a great remedy, so grab your child and share a beautiful hug and breathe in the good feeling. Kids love to be hugged.

Massage

The skin-to-skin contact that you receive from having a massage is very important to our wellbeing. Regular deep tissue massages help to break down cortisol that is stored in the body, as a result of stress.

Depression

There have been times, as Alice did in her Wonderland, I too fell into my very own rabbit hole – although unlike Alice, it was my mind that fell into a dark hole.

Depression makes no real sense and it is difficult to understand where the extreme negative emotions stem from. I am generally a happy person, who walks through life on the path of optimism and with a smile upon my face. Coming to terms and overcoming the moments of dark depression were challenging. In a depressed state, I noticed the intense lack of self-love. I didn't really want to partake of life, I longed to sleep and never really get out of bed. I was avoiding my life, I was avoiding living! I had stopped caring for me. I felt worthless, as though I had nothing to offer anyone or anything. My dark feelings stemmed from heartbreak and a total lack of self-love, the result of being in an abusive, controlling atmosphere. Part of my cure was to take care of me and the more love and self-nurture I could give myself, the more the strong grip of depression eased.

If you are experiencing any form of depression it is very advisable to seek professional help, so that you may be helped to regain the desire to live fully again and enjoy of your life. There are many different types of depression and it can be triggered by a multitude of reasons. There is nothing to be ashamed of by admitting that you aren't in the happiest of places. Look to the nature of the planet. Everything is always changing and eventually so will your depressed state of mind. Part of the cure to depression is recognising what is going on within yourself and reacting to it, to then lifting yourself up again before you fall down that hole of despair.

What Is Depression?

Depression is often compared to living in a black hole. The feelings of emptiness and impending doom, lifeless, living apathetically, feeling angry, aggressive and overly reactive. It engulfs your day-to-day life, interfering with your ability to work, study, eat, sleep and have fun. You can feel overwhelmed with feelings of helplessness, hopelessness and worthlessness.

Signs of Depression

- A bleak outlook. You no longer control negative thought patterns, strong feelings of helplessness and feeling generally as if all is hopeless
- Weight gain or loss. Having a loss of appetite or overeating, a 5% change in weight over a month

- Loss of interest in daily life. You feel like you don't want to connect to anything, you don't care
- Self-loathing. Strong feelings of worthlessness or guilt, you believe that everything is your fault
- Sleep, or oversleeping, suffering from insomnia or constantly waking throughout the night
- Your tolerance level is low. Suffering from irritability, short fuse, aggressive, everyone gets on your nerves
- Loss of energy. Suffering with fatigue, feeling sluggish, physically drained, feeling very heavy and finding small tasks very draining
- Reckless behaviour. You are starting to engage in escapist activities, alcohol, drugs, gambling, driving irresponsibly because you believe your life has no value
- Trouble focusing. Making decisions, having problems remembering things
- Aches and pains. Increased physical pain and complaints, headaches, back pain, aching muscles, stomach
- Suicidal thoughts. Wanting to end your life, because you believe everyone would be better off without you, that life holds nothing for you.

Depression in Women

Depression is twice as high in women as it is in men. A lot of this could be connected to hormonal factors, premenstrual syndrome, premenstrual dysphonic disorder, postpartum depression (baby blues) and pre-menopausal depression. Women are also more likely to suffer with seasonal light affective disorder. The symptoms that women more commonly share because of depression are over or under eating, weight gain, sleep disorders and excessive guilt.

Causes of Depression

- Loneliness
- Lack of social support

- Lack of Spiritual Faith
- Recent stressful life experiences
- Family history of depression
- Financial strain
- Early childhood trauma and abuse
- Alcohol and drug abuse
- Marital or relationship problems
- Unemployment
- Health problems and chronic pains

Helping with Depression

By simply understanding the underlying cause of your depression, you can get clear insight as to how to overcome the depressed state of being. For example, if the problem is your job, start looking for alternative employment.

Ask for help and support. Speak with your friends or family about how you are feeling so that they may offer you the support that you need. Isolation only fuels depression. It is important to connect with others. There are many helplines and supportive group environments that you can try.

Make healthy lifestyle choices. Regular exercise routines, good sleep patterns, eating healthy foods that boast your happiness levels, taking supplements for depression (Vitamin B Complex, St John's Wart etc), practise relaxation techniques, manage stress, cultivate supportive relationships and challenge negative thought patterns.

Build emotional skills. Recognising and expressing your emotions can make you feel much more resilient and build up your confidence.

Hobbies and Activities that bring joy. Do things that boost your mood and spend time in the magic of nature.

Seek professional help. Speak to a mental health professional, try a form of therapy, try alternative therapies or try medicine. Anti-depressants can relieve the symptoms of depression in some, yet they aren't the long-term cure. If you feel like you need those for the short-term, speak with your GP.

Therapy can give you the tools to treat depression from a variety of different angles. A therapist can help you to gain clear insight into the root cause of the depression, so that you may prevent it from returning. They can teach you techniques on how to move on from negative thinking and how to understand the triggers that make you feel a certain way. There are many alternative therapies available, homeopathy, hands on healing, meditation, spiritual teachings, flower essences, tapping, colour therapy and past life regression. These therapies have something positive to offer.

CHAPTER 9

Heartbreak Hotel

When any relationship dies, there is a grief process to go through, much the same as though it was a physical death. However, unlike a physical death the problems and pain that lead to the separation need to be addressed and processed.

In intimate relationships, we have bound ourselves to one another. We wear symbolic jewellery, we have taken vows, opened our hearts to one another in trust and love, we have shared our inner most secrets and planned a future. Our lives have been energetically intertwined on a deep and intimate level for some time with that person. A history is there and a past where 'death do us part' was unquestioned. If you have been together for a while, separating, breaking up is often like a surgical procedure. You must let go, which is not always easy. Letting go frees you to the wonders that may walk into your future.

So, what causes a marriage or relationship to go from the giddy highs of love to crash and burn? It's probably a cocktail of things. Relationships need maintaining, and as with everything on this earth, we are all evolving and changing constantly. Sometimes we get bogged down with daily life and don't pay enough attention to our respective other halves and they to you. We stop knowing one another and how we are individually feeling.

Communication is paramount to the success of any relationship, to understand any underlying grievances. If they are not acknowledged, these irritations seep into your relationship overshadowing the happiness. A minor problem can then start to snowball and can become

73

the elephant in the room, if not dealt with openly. I would always advise some form of marriage guidance if there is a spark of love and hope left in your marriage and you are both willing to work on your unity, before you call time on it.

Post-separation symptoms of heartbreak

- Depression
- Betrayed
- Anger
- Grief
- Unworthiness
- Humiliation
- Rejection

Healing a Broken Heart

There is no denying that break-ups are traumatic. It's hard to know that the love you once shared is no longer there. A relationship break-up can uproot all your buried insecurities and make you feel truly awful. You can and must get back to the stage in your life where you can learn to love again. First you must heal the pain and the way you do so is by learning to love yourself. The void that often shows itself after a lost love becomes filled again with your own uniquely delicious flavour of self-love. I know that with the responsibility of children, it is often hard to process your emotions. Drawing from my own personal experience, during the day I could put a happy mask on and keep it together for the sake of my daughter and employers. Yet when the flat was quiet in the evening, I would put the sad songs on and let the tears of sorrow, loneliness and worry out. And oh boy, did they flow. Acknowledging the pain made it disperse and after every teary encounter, I would feel a bit freer and stronger.

Here are 10 little tips for moving forward after a broken heart

Time – Leave the relationship in the past, it is behind you. Live within the present moment. Look forward to your new future, spend time visualising what you would like to come your way. Just don't spend too much time dwelling on the past, so that it controls your present happiness.

You – The relationship that you have with yourself is the most important. Treat yourself as you would a beloved partner. Buy yourself flowers, make you and your happiness your mission. Find the peace with your own company - love yourself.

Don't be friends with your ex immediately – Take some time out, so that you can re-establish the new boundaries with your ex. Be friends when you are ready and by that I mean you won't fall apart when he or she starts seeing someone else.

Grief – Grief is a process to go through. Don't get stuck in the emotion for too long. Take regular steps towards being happy again and you will make it.

Self-Inquiry – Just check in with your feelings towards your ex – for example do you want him back? Are you hoping that he will return to you, begging for forgiveness? Until you accept that it is really over, you can't move anywhere, you are stuck in limbo.

Let Go – Letting go isn't always easy, but for your own peace of mind you need to. Your former partner has chosen to go it alone, and that is their choice. Don't waste your time obsessing about what they are up to, checking them out on Facebook or messaging them. It is painfully self-perpetuating and won't make you feel any better. Let them go and walk on with your head held high.

Feel the Pain – Give yourself the time and permission to feel the pain, the hurt, the betrayal – whatever the emotions are that are going on – release time. Maybe crying, chatting to someone, or writing. Believe me, these emotions are better out than in.

Focus on the can do's– Give your attention to the things that you can do. Try to think positively. Start by creating a new world for yourself. Step out of the world that you once shared together, meet new people, form new friendships and make new connections. Initially it may feel a little overwhelming. However, it changes your environment from the reminders of your ex and welcomes new and delightful people into a new phase of your life.

Revel in your new independence – Be optimistic, do the things you enjoy doing – this will really help to build up your self-esteem.

Learn to trust again – So that you can allow yourself to experience the pleasures of love and intimacy again. Don't let the fear of feeling pain stop you from trusting yourself to fall in love again.

Forgiveness is perhaps the most powerful tool to mend a broken heart. To begin with, it may feel impossible to forgive someone whom has hurt you. Yet what is it to forgive? It is to stop feeling angry or resentful towards someone for an offence or mistake that they have made towards you that has caused you to hurt. In forgiving someone, you are setting yourself free from holding on to negative feelings, such as blame. Blame takes away your own personal power and gives it to the one who had wronged you. As we go through life, we all make mistakes. We all act a bit mindlessly at times, living is a learning process and mistakes happen.

Apart from forgiving another, check in with yourself. Do you need a healthy dose of self-forgiveness? Are you holding on to the mistakes that you made within the relationship? Speaking personally, I had a massive hang-up with myself for leaving my daughter virtually fatherless. I couldn't understand what I had done that was so bad within my marriage to invoke such an aggressive side in someone. I felt bad and blamed myself tirelessly. It wasn't until I was able to think rationally that I could forgive myself and then I was able to move to a happier place, where the future looked promising.

So, forgive those whom have wronged you and most importantly forgive yourself, you deserve it. Because you are worth so much more than blame.

Writing it out and getting on

A great way to get pent-up emotions out, without the necessity to share with another, is writing. This practice is ironically called writing pages – I learnt it during some therapy sessions that I attended. Every morning when you wake, just start writing approximately three A4 pages. You can do this for about four weeks plus, if needed.

All you require is a lined A4 book and a pen. Then simply start writing all your confusions, hurts, worries, betrayals and frustrations out. You don't ever need to re-read it. You don't need to worry about punctuation in what you write. It doesn't matter how angry or dark it is, or even about the neatness of your handwriting. Just write. It is a mental and emotional purging. Keep the book safe so you don't feel vulnerable of others seeing your inner turmoil.

When you feel you have written enough, just burn it – safely of course. Let it all go up in a puff of smoke! And then it's gone, all the negativity and turmoil that you have been carrying around in your mind has been let go. I found it helpful to my moving-on process. If you feel that you would like to try it, it really is a great tool to decluttering your mind.

Talking through the drama

Talking is a wonderful cure and it's a blessing to have those to listen to you. Be mindful that you don't make your problems the focus of all the conversations. Friends and family will support you, but if they don't see you willing to move on, it can be draining for them too. Talking to a councillor can be beneficial. They are impartial and their connection to you is purely professional. By listening to you, they can give you inner insights from picking up on your behavioural story. This can then highlight your patterns.

Laughter

Don't underestimate the power of laughter. You can't stay sad for long if you laugh. Laughter is probably the best cures for wellbeing. It engages your physical body, as well as connecting to the brain, promoting a feel-good chemical reaction. Find your laughter trigger and when you aren't feeling the love for life, go to that place – if it's a scene from a film, an experience, a joke, a story, or just your own wacky sense of humour. Laugh and enjoy laughing. Life can be far too stressful at times and in this stress-induced state of being we forget the simplicity of laughter. Self-induced laughter also works. You just make yourself laugh until you stop trying – this is yoga laughter.

CHAPTER 10

The Relationship With Yourself

The relationship you have with yourself, is often reflected in the relationships you have externally. All relationships are mirrors of the way you are. How you behave, how you think and how you feel.

You attract what you put out. For example, if you are feeling vibrant and enthused by life you attract many great experiences and people. If you are stuck in a negative mind-set and spend your time negatively criticising everything, you will find that happy people want to run in the opposite direction to you and that you will be stuck in a place of discontented limbo.

Relationships on a close level can identify inner parts of you, both good and bad, that you have not connected to previously. The more you love yourself, the more love and respect you attract. Sharing from my own marriage relationship experience, I can show you an example of what I mean. As previously mentioned, I was in an abusive relationship. Initially my husband wasn't physically abusive, there was controlling behaviour and verbal putdowns to begin with, which I swallowed, as I believed them. My husband was a very charismatic man, who was outwardly fun, generous, caring and he was liked. My people-pleasing and 'putting myself second' habit allowed him to continue the putdowns and control, which made me question myself constantly, in self-doubt and self-deprecation. If I had held myself with greater respect and love, then I would have nipped the relationship in the bud much earlier than

I did. In essence I probably wouldn't have attracted a man with such a dark side in the first place.

Coming out from the marriage, I had to do a lot of self-reflection, letting go and healing, before I could fully journey through the gateway of 'self-love'. It was a conscious choice that I made as I want future relationships to be magical.

The Journey to Self-Love

Self-love is attained by self-nurture and self-respect.

Recognise that you are amazing. It is not always easy to think this. We often think that it is an ego projection and feel uncomfortable with holding ourselves in high esteem. Self-love is an inner depth of respect that we have for ourselves. It comes from within, it is beyond the ego. You are amazing, your children would be the first to agree and I am sure there would be many more who would join the queue to agree. Don't let one negative event or person's inconsiderate actions towards you change the way you feel about yourself. Surround yourself with people who make you feel good and those who can be lovingly honest with you. Look at all the amazing things that you do – being a parent is amazing.

Write a list of the reasons to love yourself and then a list of reasons for you not to love yourself. The list of reasons for you not to love yourself can be changed, if you don't love yourself because of bad habits and patterns, you can change these. Self-development work takes time and effort, but it really works at shifting deep-seated negative beliefs that we may be holding onto about ourselves.

Don't stop loving yourself because you have a few more lines than you did at 20, or that you have a few grey hairs. This is just the natural cycle of life. If you don't love yourself because of past actions, then learn from them and forgive. If you feel that you are unlovable because you are a bit overweight, you can change that. Eating right and exercising are companions on the journey to self-love. Your body loves to move through exercise and it loves to be fed food, which makes it feel vibrant. Always focus on the reasons to love you and your insecurities will fall away and you will be shine from your inner glow.

Self-Worth

Value yourself. There is one of you. Anything unique is given priceless value. 'One' of Monet's paintings is sold for a premium. However beautiful the painting is, it is paint on canvas. You are a multi-faceted wonder of uniqueness, with no price tag, making you priceless. Your worth is far greater than maybe you can perceive, but keep trying to grab a hold of that concept. Adopt a grateful mind-set for who you are and all the wonderful things that you have in your life.

Affirmations

These are powerful short sentences that affirm something positive to us. They are powerful statements of change. By saying, hearing or even listening to affirmations they become your thoughts. Each day we have thousands upon thousands of thoughts, many of which are negative. By repeating affirmations we are consciously controlling our thoughts, which helps to change our reality and what we attract into our life. It sounds too simple to work – a group of words – yet they are wonderfully effective. Internally repeating the appropriate statement can help with the way we see ourselves, how we behave, how we feel and what we attract materially and romantically.

Examples Affirmations

General:
I am a success in all that I do
I feel happy, I feel healthy, I feel terrific
Everything feels just right

Financial Abundance:
I am a money magnet
I prosper wherever I turn and I know that I deserve prosperity of
    all kinds
I pay my bills with love, as I know abundance flows freely through me

Health:
Every cell in my body vibrates with energy and health
My body heals quickly and easily

Weight loss:
I am the perfect weight for me
I choose to make positive healthy choices for myself
I accept myself unconditionally right now

Self Esteem:
When I believe in myself others do
I am my own unique self, special, creative and wonderful

Joy:
Life is joyfully filled with delightful surprises
I choose, love, joy and freedom, open my heart and allow wonderful
things to flow into my life

Peace:
I am at peace
I trust in the process of life

Romance:
I release any desperation and allow love to find me
I attract only healthy relationships

Love:
I know that I deserve love and accept it now
I give love and it is returned to me multiplied

Positive Projection

See yourself and your life how you want it to become, almost as
though it has become that already. That can be physically, mentally,
emotionally, spiritually, your career, your living arrangements, or future
relationships. Make a destination and keep visualising it, manifesting

the change. If you see yourself as a fatty, you are never going to slim down because you hold that picture of yourself in your head. Visualise yourself as everything that you want to be, everything that you truly are. Avoid perfectionist thoughts – aim to where is realistic.

Self-love activities

Do things that make you happy. Practise the things that you have loved doing, or find new interests that you feel drawn too. Make time to see friends and attend social gatherings, so that you are out there and enjoying life.

Taking responsibility for the way you feel

Owning your feelings allows you to change, so that you are no longer a repeat offender. If you feel tired, take action by going to sleep early. Don't just moan about it, as that cures nothing apart from giving yourself a headache. If you feel great, own that too.

Self-maintenance

Taking good care of your body is paramount to feeling great about yourself. It is a lovely way to self-nurture. When we feel good about our physical appearance, we automatically feel more confident and happy. As a busy parent, it is often all about the giving, so it is important that you give to you too – book yourself in for a pedicure, a manicure, a haircut, a facial, a massage. Open the door to 'I deserve and am worth some me time'. Take time to have a long relaxing bubble bath. Cook yourself your favourite dinner. Go on a lovely walk.

Always smile at your reflection in the mirror. Don't think unkind thoughts about yourself, you are on a journey of recapturing self-love and that is very often achieved by accepting yourselves for who and how you are.

If you are fed up with your wardrobe and your hairdo, give yourself a makeover. Get rid of the clothes that make you feel frumpy, fat and those clothes that no longer do you justice. Charity shops are always grateful for donations. You may also be able to do wardrobe swaps with friends. Find a style and colour palette that suits you and work towards transforming your wardrobe. Call in the help of a ruthlessly honest friend, if you have attachment issues. I always think it is a very good idea to own an outfit that makes you feel beyond magnificent and you should have one for every season.

Reclaiming your identity

When my daughter was born, people stopped seeing me as me. I just became my daughter's mother. It was funny. They would coo around the pushchair, asking questions, often not even making eye contact. It happens. I love being my daughter's mother, it's a big honour, but I am also me. Being invisible isn't good for anyone's self-esteem, so make sure that you reclaim your identity. And the best way to do that is to sometime venture out without your children, socialise, let people get to know YOU and what makes you tick. Allow yourself to know yourself once again.

If you have just come out of relationship, you are no longer part of the pairing that the world has witnessed, for as many years as you were together. You are forced to walk alone and that can feel a little unnatural. Don't stay hidden in the shadows. Let the world see you as an individual once again. It does sometimes take a big cup of courage to walk into an event or gathering when you are newly alone. I felt like a failure after my marriage crumbled and I stupidly believed that others were judging me harshly. Of course they weren't. Over time you get used to it and it no longer bothers you. Being single lets you mingle freely with so many new people and there are so many interesting folks to meet. It's in these little times, when you are happy and completely content with being you, that you will attract a new partner who is also completely content with you being you!

Life Detox

Sometimes we all need to detox our life. Detoxing helps to make you to feel good, as it lightens your load. Get rid of ill-fitting garments, old lotions, potions and make up, old kitchen cupboards items, toxic friends and situations, and old hoarded clutter. Our physical bodies also benefit from a seasonal cleanse, to help to keep them working at their optimum level. It's also a good time to take stock of the mental and emotional baggage that you are carrying around, so that you may move on to a new phase within yourself. If there are aspects of your life that are no longer working, use this detox time to re-evaluate and take positive steps to make the changes needed.

A few months into my newly-single life, I detoxed my house and my life of my ex. I didn't get rid of everything that we ever bought together, but I did get rid of stuff that didn't make me feel peaceful or happy. I shipped things off to the charity shop, the dump, put papers through the shredder and my wedding ring disappeared into nearby bushes. It was a fresh start for me and a new beginning. I didn't want material reminders of our marriage everywhere I looked. Getting rid of things is ceremoniously letting go of the past, encouraging new things to come in to your life.

Home Detox

Over weeks, months and years we accumulate stuff – be it paper, old mail, magazines, old cleaning products, old tins of paint, out-of-date food and beauty products, treasured items which no longer hold their original magic, clothes or old linen. Rather than keeping it, taking up space the less stuff that you have lying around your home, the easier it will be to manage. If you haven't worn something for a couple of years, then get rid of it (unless it has huge sentimental value to you). Ditto for old toys, outgrown children's books, things that serve no use or need any longer.

Physical Detox

Try cutting out or really reducing your intake of alcohol, sugar, dairy, wheat and animal products for five days. Drink plenty of water, natural herbal teas, fresh vegetable juices and fruit smoothies. Eat a large variety of vegetables and fruits, whole grains and pulses. If you go to your local health food shops they will sell herbal tonics that will assist you in purging your system. It is advisable to do detoxes as the seasons change, especially spring and autumn, and ideally around the time of the new moon. Commence a detox when you feel mentally ready – there is no point in starting something if you are not really or in the right frame of mind, as the last thing you want to do is feel that you failed. You can always try one day at a time and gradually build it up. Cleansing through elimination is great at helping to break bad dietary habits.

Friend detox

This can seem quite cruel, but for your own wellbeing you need to surround yourself with people who can be honest with you and those that have your best interests at heart. Those who criticise you, dump their problems on you and are never there for when you need them aren't people who are ever going to make you feel great. Friendship is all about balance, about give and take. You don't need to exterminate these people from your life, just put some distance between you and them.

Alternative therapies

There is such an array of holistic therapies available which can help you on many levels to get rid of old held-onto beliefs, behavioural patterns and destructive habits. In the spirit of your detox, visit a therapist who can help you address the problems in hand.

Aromatherapy

This is a type of alternative therapy that uses essential oils and other aromatic plant compounds to improve your mood. The inhalation of essential oils stimulates the part of the brain connected to smell, causing chemicals to be released making the person feel relaxed, calm and even stimulated. Aromatherapy massages deepen the relaxation. Aromatherapy oils also can have anti-viral, anti-fungal, antiseptic and anti-bacterial properties.

Flower essences can really help to shift old emotional and mental patterns. If you do decide to use them, be sure to drink lots of water – it helps. You will really feel the benefits of clearing out the old.

Thai Oil Massage

These are wonderful deep massages. The therapist can release tension held deep within the muscles and it's great for detoxing. I always feel a sense of peace and sleep beautifully well afterwards.

NLP

Neuro-linguistic Programming is a short-term, goal-orientated approach to therapy for problem-solving. It can help with coping with stress, anger management, anxiety, improving performance, pain management and weight issues. It is empowering and can help you to overcome negative thought and belief patterns, lack of confidence and destructive relationship patterns. It can help you deal with break-ups and is successful in bereavement counselling.

Homeopathy

As with all holistic therapies, homeopathy works on the whole being – mind, body, spirit. It is a vibrational treatment. The remedy is matched to the ailment using the 'like to heal like' principle. Homoeopathy can help with physical ailments as well as emotional. It's incredibly effective.

Nutritionist

A nutritionist can guide you back to optimum health, by suggesting changes that you should make to your diet, they can identify food sensitivities and vitamin deficiencies. If you are wanting to improve your diet for health and weight reasons they are very encouraging and supportive offering you dietary insight and recipe suggestions.

Chiropractor for back skeletal issues

Don't underestimate the back. It supports us to stand up straight. A good posture gives us the knowing of having a backbone (as in courage and self-pride). When your back is aligned in the way nature intended, your sense of wellbeing is really improved. The spine has all the body's nerves running through it, transmitting information from the brain stem to the rest of the body, if your back is out of alignment, causing pinching to the nerves, it will be the cause of chronic or acute backache, headaches, aches and pains, physical tension and bad sleep patterns. The chiropractor painlessly realigns the out of place vertebrae, by a gentle manipulation. You should be given exercises and advice to help you strengthen the muscles that support your spine.

Detox Your Worries

Worrying doesn't take away tomorrows troubles, it just takes away today's peace. Worrying is living in a worst-case scenario. If you are worried about your health, for example, go and see a health practitioner. If there is something wrong it can be investigated, diagnosed and cured. Worrying about something that hasn't been diagnosed is unnecessary. The only positive is that health scares can propel us into taking better care of ourselves and not to take our bodies for granted. Booking an appointment with the doctor and getting your bloods done can just help you to know the state of your health. Finding the solutions to any of your concerns starts by contacting the people who have expertise in that field.

Little Detox Ideas for Everyday Life

A cup of Nettle Tea (a blood purifier) once a day. Drink a large glass of warm water and lemon juice every morning, to get your organs going. Fast for one day a month. This gives your digestive system a break, even if it's a mini-fast 6 p.m. to 9 a.m. the following day. Eat at least six servings of fruit and vegetables a day, as raw as possible.

Body Brushing is an effective way to get the body's lymphatic system working effectively. The lymphatic helps to remove the toxins from our body. With body brushing you simply start from the feet and brush all the way up to your heart and similarly do it from your hands to your heart, your neck downwards again, to your heart. Body brushing helps with reducing cellulite and brightens your skin.

Take a Sea Salt or Epsom Salt bath, or soak your feet in a salted foot bath with your favourite essential oils. Salt baths are great for stress relief, muscle and joint aches, improving circulation, headache relief, and helps with mineral absorption and improves sleep.

Make a salt scrub. Easy and cheap to make at home, all you need is an odourless, cold pressed oil – sesame or sunflower seed oil are ideal – fine sea salt, and your favourite essential oils. Good essential oil combinations are grapefruit, ginger and tangerine, yalang yalang, geranium and orange, geranium, basil and lime, peppermint, eucalyptus and lavender or rose, jasmine and clary sage.

Moisturise your skin regularly and make time to give yourself mini-manicures and pedicures.

Sit up with a straight back and stand proud. This will give all your internal organs room to expand. A good posture is an attractive asset.

Every spiritual master will advise meditation for a quieter mind. Meditation helps us to centre and reconnect with the truth within, not to the jumbling jumping mind. There are many different methods of meditation, repetitive mantra chanting, silent meditation and healing visualisation meditation. For beginners, I suggest sitting down for five minutes (which you may gradually increase) in a relaxed and comfortable environment. Close your eyes, take five deep breathes and really focus your attention on your breathing. Let the breath feel your entire body, then normalise your breathing and focus your attention solely on your in-breath and out-breath. After each in-breath hold it for the count of five before exhaling. After exhaling, count to five before inhaling. You can meditate any time of the day – on waking or before sleep are the best.

Turn the TV off and do something creative or visualise your dreams. Take positive steps to make your daydreams a reality. Even if it's just research, taking the first steps in the direction you want your life to go towards, starts the ball of change rolling.

Have a non-phone, non-Facebook, non-email, non-twitter day – it's liberating.

Don't spend money for one day. We live in such a material and consumer-driven world that not spending money for a day is such a welcome change. If you can do a day, try doing it for two days in a row. The money that you save can go towards a special outing.

Don't drive for a day. Give your car a rest and your legs a walk-out. There are positives, as it saves on your fuel bill and gives you a good bit of exercise. Go for a walk in nature and really be aware of your beautiful surroundings.

Have an early night. Set yourself a time and then go to bed. Read, relax and think happy thoughts. A good night's sleep is a tonic.

Break away from routine and go on a spontaneous day out. You choose, or let the kids choose. Just give yourselves the freedom to roam and enjoy some time out.

Introducing New Patterns and Breaking Old Habits

To have a good intention is one thing. To implement it into your daily life is a great thing, as well as being a great achievement.

The key to forming any habit is repetition. Whether it is a positive or negative habit, it's all about doing something regularly, so that it becomes second nature. Like brushing our teeth, for example. We know that for healthy teeth and gums, and a fresh breath, cleaning teeth is important. If you forget to clean your teeth you know it, you feel it and you taste it. Smoking, junk food, alcohol, drugs-taking are initially habits, however the mind becomes addicted to the multitude of chemicals that are present in them, giving you the high. This makes giving them up more challenging, but not impossible. Compulsive shopping, gambling or sexual addiction is a different form of habitual addiction. You become addicted to the way it makes you feel, the risk, and the adrenaline high.

Addictions and self-destructive habits can be overcome, when you have enough self-love and self-respect to want something better for yourself. I used to smoke and drink far too much in my early twenties. One day whilst nursing my very pained sick body, I thought "Wow, I can't feel like this anymore". I was repetitively destroying myself. In that moment, I decided to quit smoking and drinking. It wasn't easy, but since then I have never had a puff of a cigarette, neither do I rely on alcohol to make me feel good. Drinking alcohol is something that I can now do in moderation, or can leave all together.

Strengthening your willpower and taking responsibility for yourself is a good thing. Replace unhealthy ways with healthy alternatives and focus on the new alternative, rather than what you are giving up. When you feel an urge rising from within, quickly refocus your mind.

If you are struggling to overcome a negative behavioural pattern, seek professional help. They will be able to offer you the support and encouragement to keep going and often will be able to identify the root cause and work with you to overcome it.

To introduce a new habit, do it every day for 21 days. If it is getting outside for a walk, do it regularly for 21 days. You will feel the benefit and it will then become part of your day-to-day routine. Just as cleaning your teeth did. Just keep pushing through the resistance barrier and know that you will reap the benefits. 21 days is the key... And what an achievement you will have made!

Tapping – what is it and how it works...

Tapping is a blend of techniques, marrying the wisdom of the Ancient Chinese acupressure with modern psychology. Tapping is simple and painless, extremely effective and is very accessible as it can be practised by anyone who feels called to try it. It works by tapping on certain points along our bodies' meridians, as seen in the diagram, whilst saying a statement that is relevant to your emotions, experience or pain that has arisen.

Meridians are the energy pathways that our bodies' energy flows through along a specific network of channels. By tapping on these nine specific points we can release negative feelings and reactions, as acupoints talk to the 'amygdala' - a part of our brain that initiates our bodies' negative reaction to fear. Tapping is a technique that can set us free from our negative reactions to certain circumstances and beliefs. It is super effective in alleviating issues like depression, anxiety, insomnia, negative emotions (anger jealousy, sadness, fear), painful and traumatic memories, unresolved problems and unbalanced emotions. It can even help to aliviate the effects of persistent negative messages we may have received from key people in our lives such as parents, teachers or spouses etc.

EFT TAPPING POINTS

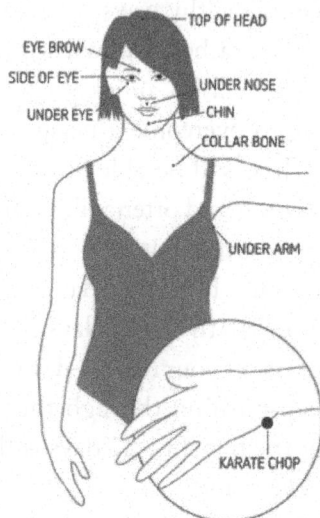

TOP OF HEAD
EYE BROW
SIDE OF EYE
UNDER EYE
UNDER NOSE
CHIN
COLLAR BONE
UNDER ARM
KARATE CHOP

The basic technique

I am just going to touch on this subject to give you a brief insight. For more information, please do research it. Nick Ortner is a very passionate master of tapping and I would highly recommend his book.

To begin with

Firstly, you must focus on the negative emotion that has arisen within you—a fear, an anxiety, a bad experience, a difficult emotional reaction to something, frustration etc. (NB - Tapping also works on physical pain.)

Whilst focusing on the emotion, you then come up with a verbal statement which you say 3 times whilst tapping on the point on the side of the hand known as the karate chop.

Each statement ends with "I deeply and completely love myself"

Examples of verbal statements

You first tap on the point known as the karate chop. Seven to nine times on the karate, whilst saying the set-up statement three times, using your index and middle fingers.

NB – the statement is in bold, the reminder phrase is underlined and the reframe statement to go with the set-up statement is in italic

Even though I feel that I am not ok as I am, I deeply and completely love and accept myself
<u>I am not feeling ok</u>
I am perfect as I am

Even though I am afraid that I cannot cope, I deeply and completely love and accept myself
<u>I am afraid I am not coping</u>
I am safe and coping

Even though I feel depressed and helpless, I deeply love and completely love myself
I am depressed and helpless
I can take care of myself

Even though I feel angry I deeply and completely love and accept myself
I feel angry
I am at peace

Even though I feel like I am failing I completely love and accept myself
I am failing
I am doing well

Even though I feel that I am not worthy of love I completely love and accept myself
I feel unworthy
I am loved

Even though I feel let down I completely love and accept myself
I have been let down
I end relationships that cannot be healthy

Even though I feel that I must jump through hoops for love I deeply and completely love myself
I try so hard to be loved
I am true to myself

Even though I feel over whelmed and alone I deeply and completely love myself
I am lonely and out of my depth
I am safe and loved

Even though I have this headache I deeply love and accept myself
I have a killer headache
I feel great

You can create your own set up statement to match your chosen issue:

Even though I feel (personalise) I deeply and completely love myself.
I feel (feeling)
I am (personalise)

After tapping on the karate chop three times using the set-up statement, you then move to the top of the head, eyebrow, side of eye, under eye, under nose, chin, collar bone and finally under the arm. On each point you tap 7 times saying a reminder phase.

Once you have done a round of the tapping see how you feel. Is the emotion still feeling as intense? If so, repeat until it feels less intense, I usually do it twice, then on the third round I say the reframe statement.

CHAPTER 11

The Power Of Flower

Flower Power Remedies

In times of emotional and mental stress, I would recommend flower remedies as a safe and alternative use to allopathic medicine. They are amazing and speaking personally I have had very liberating experiences from using them.

Flower remedies are a vibrational medicine. If your knowledge of vibrational medicines is limited, let me explain briefly. Vibrational medicines work on the principle that we are all physical manifestations of vibrating energy. When we are happy, for example, our energies vibrate quickly with flow and grace. When we are sad we feel a physical heaviness within our bodies. So in short, our reaction to experiences affects the way we vibrate. As humans, we are emotional beings and negative experiences can become stuck within us, causing toxic thought patterns and reactions to form.

If you can, imagine your body as a flowing river, and hurts, unforgiveness, fear, anger, insecurities, dependencies, jealousy, sorrows and lack of self-worth are blocks along that river that are stopping its natural flow. Flower remedies work magically on the blocks that are stopping your natural mojo flowing in a thriving way, through their vibration. This helps to disburse the blocks. You may experience a little intensity from the release, yet this is a great sign that the remedies are working the way nature intended.

The creators of the flower remedies have an innate resonance to the plant kingdom, they have spent time observing the flowers' energy and their healing potentials. They have observed the flowers, plants, trees at a greater level than just the immediate beauty and scent and have recognised the true vibration they hold within and how they can be used medicinally to help us heal.

For all those non-believers, that's fine, you don't have to take my word for it, but if you are looking for something to help you feel better, you have nothing really to lose in trying flower remedies.

I use a brand called Bailey Flower Essences. It has a wide selection to choose from and its combination remedies are often ideal, as they encompass the basics. There are flower remedy practitioners who would be able to combine individual remedies to suit your story and individual need. Flower remedies aren't medicines in the conventional sense and they are not intended to cure or alleviate medical conditions. If you are in doubt, always contact a medical practitioner. Flower remedies are catalysts for inner change.

Composite Essences

Flower essences come in their individual flower forms, or they can be purchased in composites, which are a blend of individual essences that work together on specific emotions. Examples are listed below.

Anger and Frustration

These balance and stabilise our fire energies, so that we can take proper control of our lives. We all need energy. If too much energy is expressed, we become angry. If there is too little we can become ineffective. We need our energy to be in balance. This composite helps us to achieve that in several ways. This remedy helps us to live our lives more fully, as we become more able to take control of our emotional reactions to the situations we meet.

Childhood

Most if not all of us have difficulties in life that have their roots in our childhood experiences and conditioning. They can last right through our adult lives. The difficulty is that these deeply-implanted, conditioned patterns can even take over our lives from time to time, depending on what triggers them. We can then behave completely out of character – afterwards we must deal with the consequences of our actions. This composite essence helps us 'to come up to date' by gradually dissolving those patterns.

Confusion

When we become confused, our minds tend to be overactive, trying to find a way out, yet continually coming up against obstacles. This composite essence helps us to relax and take a more detached view of our present difficulties, so that we can see clearly what we should be doing.

Dependency

There are times in everyone's life when we become very dependent on something or someone. The difficulty with all such dependencies is that they restrict our freedom to act. Indeed, we can become slaves to the situation. This composite essence helps to break up over dependant patterns.

Depression and Despair

It can be easy to feel depressed at times when things seem to be negative and beyond our control. If we hit a horrendous situation, this can turn into despair. This essence tackles those times when we become locked in negative thought patterns in several different ways.

Fears

Fears can inhibit so much of our lives and can often be difficult to eradicate. They deny us much of our freedom and enjoyment in life. The intention behind this essence is to bring our fears out into the open where they can be seen for what they really are – 'paper tigers' that look ferocious when hidden in dark corners, but in fact have no real power or substance. Deeply-rooted fears can date back to childhood and so the childhood essence can often help when given at the same time.

Grief

When we suffer from bereavement of the loss of something precious in our lives, we need to be able to express our grief so that it does not become locked within us.

Liberation

To dissolve our emotional attachment to objects, events and people. This essence is for those who have become trapped by their circumstances. It may be that there is a dominant friend or partner who is causing the difficulties. They do not feel in charge of their own lives.

Obsession

For when a particular thought just keeps going around and round and will not go away. The 'mouse on the treadmill' type of feeling, with each thought following relentlessly on the heels of another. The thought itself seems to provide the momentum.

Sadness and Loneliness

For those times when we need comfort, love and reassurance – or to encourage new beginnings. Sadness and loneliness can have a devastating effect on our lives. We can feel wholly dispirited and bereft. We need a new viewpoint, a new and transforming way of seeing the world.

Self-Esteem

For those who feel disempowered, dominated by others and are unable to assert themselves in the world, or suffer from blocked-off self-love. Many people suffer from low self-esteem and it does not always show up as subservience. Over-aggressive behaviour shows a lack of self-esteem just as surely.

Shock and Trauma

This is the essence of choice for sudden or long-term shock or trauma. When circumstances around us suddenly change, we can become very shocked. Whatever the causes, three things are needed to help us emerge from our traumas as rapidly and easily as possible. These are covered by three essences.

Tranquillity

This brings peace to the overactive mind. It helps to empower us, by bringing us into the present moment. Many of us do not lead a tranquil life. We are always active and do not find peace within that busyness. This essence encourages us to change our attitude to life and to find peace within the storms of everyday life. It does not force change on us.

Transition

This composite is designed to help those who are having trouble because of major changes in their lives. Whether those changes seem to be good or bad, such times can be extremely stressful. Nevertheless, the past needs to make way for the new and the composite can help with that.

For my daughter, I use the Indigo Essence brand. These were remedies created by a homeopath with the guidance of bright young children. They have proven to work time and time again with my daughter. They are non-toxic and really help your child to balance out their emotions.

CHAPTER 12

Finding Love Again

As far as I have experienced, there seem to be no rules when it comes to love. When there is true love it just seems to flow, it fills you with peace and joy and a sense of optimistic renewal. Love can flow of course between anyone. You don't need to be intimately involved with someone to experience love –look at the love you feel for your children. Yet the journey to find this new romantic intimate love can often be a bumpy one. This is speaking from my own experience and being aware of my friends dating successes and woes.

Create with your children

All relationships are not equal, and you need to decide, what it is that, you want from a future partner. If you are after a physically intimate connection or a relationship that has potential to go the forever partnership distance.

If you are just after some intimacy, it would be advisable to leave your children out of the picture. This is so that they don't become attached and read into the relationship more than it is. Hang out and play with your new mate when they are not around. Children are not always happy with the presence of a new partner in your life. They may feel that they are losing you to another and become tricky, and play up, due to feeling insecure. They may also feel that you are replacing their mother or father – of course this isn't the case – yet children do have loyalty to both parents. Keep the lines of communication open and be as honest as you can with them. Listen to their concerns and respect what they share with you.

You and your children are a team. If it is a forever lasting relationship that you are looking for, they will play a huge part in attracting the right person to you. I often sit down with my daughter and we chat about the qualities a new man would have and what he would bring to our little family. We drew a big 'creating' picture of what, we (mum, daughter and Mr Dazzler) would all be like and feel like together as a new little family.

It was a fun exercise and it helped my daughter to feel included and see the potential in having a new man in our lives. I shared with her what I would like from my perspective – leaving the intimate bits out, because she doesn't need to know that – and she shared what she would like. It's advisable not to describe the new partner as 'new' mummy or daddy. Children will always have loyalty to their biological parent, even if they not present.

Getting Out There

When is the right time to start dating again? Well for me, I had come from a super-traumatic relationship and needed to heal and learn the lessons from that relationship. And just for the record, there is always something to learn. Whether it's knowing that you deserve better and learning to value and love yourself to levels of new highs, or whether it is taking responsibility for the part that you played with the dynamics of your marriage breakdown. Quite often both lessons are relevant.

My advice would be to take some time out from finding new love. It's very tempting to yearn for a new lover to fill the void that's been left behind. First fill that void yourself with self-love sparkles, ooze with confidence, find your sense of self and love the uniqueness of you again.

After a big heart relationship breakdown, we may experience overwhelming feelings of unworthiness, sadness and an abundance of insecurities surface. Know your self-worth, because you are so very worthy of greatness. Past is past and what has gone has gone. Forgive and then move on with your life and your children, in a happy and a beautiful way.

You will attract a real dazzler of a man if that is indeed what you wish for when the time is right. And the right time can be different for all of us. You need to exude the energy of 'I am available', as this is a big part of attracting interest.

Dating can be an emotional rollercoaster, so you need to fill yourself with supreme amounts of self-confidence, so you can stay centred and grounded. It's unlikely that you will meet your dazzler on the first date you go on – you'll probably have to go on a few dates. So make it feel fun to you, do things that you don't usually do, dress up, feel womanly (as it can be easy to get caught up in the mummy trap), enjoy meeting new friends 'with potential'. But don't be too attached to the outcome, let things develop naturally. This way you are not making yourself vulnerable to skidding down the slide of disappointment.

It's very easy to get carried away in the moment. You are feeling the renewed joy of mutual attraction, this guy ticks more boxes than you could imagine, you get on amazingly well, but he isn't ready to commit to a relationship. Hmmm, is he ever going to be? How much time and energy do you realistically want to invest? And remember it may be that he may just be unable to emotionally commit because he has got his own stuff going on, it's not a personal rejection.

You may go on dates that don't go anywhere, although you really wished they would have and vice versa. It's good to have a realistic wish list and at the top of that list should be someone who treats you as his 'dazzling queen' and your children with love, kindness and respect. The material requests should be of secondary importance.

So, to meeting new potential beaus. Where to meet someone? Do you trust in fate or do you take steps to make it happen? I like to think it is a healthy dose of both. Take the steps with faith that fate will bring the right person to you.

Firstly, be open to meeting someone new. If you aren't open, you will just put out the wrong vibes. After my separation, I wasn't ready and totally wasn't open. If I saw someone approaching me with a glint in his eyes, I would literally dive bomb behind the nearest trees or shrubbery, engage in a deep conversation promptly with someone (anyone), get up and run out the room, or just freeze in fear! I couldn't deal with anything that may have opened those wounds before they had had a chance to heal. Being ready to be open is important, so that you can receive, because it is great to receive love and kindness again.

You can meet people anywhere – in the workplace, at the gym, through hobbies, through friends, being out and about. If these are avenues that you have tried with limited success, maybe try internet dating, single's nights and dating agencies. Find an internet site that has some common ground for you. There is an abundance of dating websites out there – for meeting fellow vegetarians, classical music fans, for those who like their partners in uniforms, single parent dating sites, the list is endless. Just find the one that resonates with you. I think the key to internet dating is patience. It can sometimes feel like people are all about their ideals. Don't be shy, there is nothing to lose. If you like someone's profile, then send them an introduction.

If you feel you are out of practice on the dating front, there are classes that you can take. To build up your confidence, they teach you a few conversation pointers and can help you to get more comfortable with flirting. It can initially seem a bit overwhelming and uncomfortable, but once you become more accustomed to it, it can be a lot of fun!

Basic Flirting Tips

First you make eye contact. A few times is fine. Smile. If there is a response, then engage in a small conversation (it doesn't matter who initiates this). Ask the guy if he can help you with something that feels relevant to you, him and the environment that you are in. And before you know it, sparks can be flying and if they aren't – well, move on, you have lost nothing. He will have been flattered to have been approached by a gorgeous woman and you have had a little interaction practise.

Many of us dream of a soulmate relationship, of finding the one. What really is a soulmate relationship and who is the 'one'? A soulmate relationship in my mind is a relationship that is built on respect, trust and honesty. The love is totally unconditional, you feel a deep sense of peace and reassurance from this person, and you feel free to love to levels of renewed highs and depths. From experiencing this level of love, you can love everyone in the world a little more. Soulmate relationships aren't solely romantic – they can happen between your child, a friend, a teacher, a parent. It's a love between souls rather than personalities. It's a deep love, but that's not to say they are the easiest relationships, as the personalities may be out of sync. As they say, each relationship is a teacher.

In Madeira there is a saying: "For every foot, there is a perfect fitting shoe". If you believe that there is a soulmate or great love out there for you, then begin looking for it.

New Relationships Bringing Up the Past

When entering a new relationship, it may inevitably bring up the dormant fears of your previous relationship. This is not an abnormal reaction. In many ways it is our emotions' way of protecting us against future heartbreak. However, this is where you need to be logical and use your inner discernment. Heartbreak happens and I am sure that if you asked a hundred people on the street, they would all say that they would rather have loved and got burnt than not loved at all.

You cannot let the hurts of the past stand in your way of receiving future happiness. It really takes a lot of courage to put yourself out there and to feel your vulnerability, as you open your heart to someone new. These are perfectly normal reactions. YOU must own your past feelings of heartbreak and sit with them for a while and then let them go. Not everyone you enter a relationship with is going to hurt you.

You need to begin to trust your inner discernment, also known as your 'gut feeling'. With age and experience brings wisdom. Don't settle for less than you deserve. You will get the sense if someone has a lot of unresolved issues. In balanced relationships, there needs to be love at the core, rather than neediness, otherwise you are forming a relationship based on co-dependence.

Your new lover needs to have theirs and your best interests at heart, and you theirs. If it doesn't feel aligned, simply don't go there. Allow for someone who is worth you on many levels to come along.

If your love has been betrayed in the past, you will recognise the signs. True love gives you peace and you can feel a sense of expansion within your spirit. When something isn't right, you will feel twitchy and your emotions will feel unbalanced. Most people of a certain age have a past – that almost goes without saying. Don't bring the baggage of the past into a new relationship, but do be honest with what you've experienced, so that your new partner can empathise with you and help to settle any doubts and insecurities, that you may be experiencing.

From my personal experience, I was battered and bruised when my marriage ended. I dreamed of a romantic fairy tale, a knight in shining armour to love away all that hurt within me. That wasn't going to happen and if it did, it would have been a very unhealthy relationship, as it would have been based on need. I would always have seen him as a savour, and become over attached to him. Yet more importantly I would not have found my own inner strength, which was part of my healing journey. Aside from the Disney dream, I had been really damaged by my ex-husband and didn't really want a repeat relationship and just wanted to get my happiness back. And for a long time I didn't want or wasn't ready for a relationship.

A large part of healing my heart was meeting new men and forming close and fun friendships. They all treated me with great respect and kindness, something that had been missing in my marriage. Their presence in my life really served as a great way for me to begin to trust men again and to open my heart for Mr Dazzler.

CHAPTER 13

Your Children And Their Absent Parent

I have taken the word 'absent' and am using it in its broadest context to encompass dad not being present – whether that is at home with mum, or the fathers whom have absconded, never to be seen or heard from again, by you or their children.

If Dad or Mum Is Still Present and Willing

If dad or mum still wants contact with their children, then you would be a fool not to allow them access to that. Heartbreak can bring out the worst in us and often the children get used as pawns in a very unkind game and that is not right. In the long-term there are no winners. Put your feelings aside and do the right thing for your children. There is only a minority of fathers and mothers who don't want to continue the relationship with their child. Often, the parent that has left the family home will be really missing their children and can feel terribly lonely without their presence. It will be so important for them and your children to spend time together. Remember it's a hard time for everyone. There's a lot of adjusting, for everyone to get used to the new dynamic of the family unit.

Mums and dads have a right to see their children – and their children to see them. They are after all their parent and they need to form a lasting relationship with their offspring. For example, a father can offer a child different experiences than a mother can. It can help them to feel whole, because they have two parent to identify with. Grandparents, aunts and uncles can often be the casualties of marriage breakdowns, for a number of reasons. They no doubt will have formed special ties to your children and your children to them. Be the bigger person, rise above the blaming, the ill-feeling and hold the space in your heart, so that your children can continue to have that relationship with their extended family. Maybe it is not going to be easy to begin with. If they love your child, they will also be there to support you in bringing them up. Set your boundaries, if you feel that they are not respecting you in front of your children, then you have every right to reset the conditions.

There are many positives to having an active relationship with your children's father or mother and their wider extended family, for them and you:

- They shoulder and share some of the parenting responsibilities
- It gives you time off from being a parent, so that you may start to create a new life for you
- You have an ally to share concerns you may have about your children, whether it's schooling, unhealthy friendships, or their behaviour. Hopefully your ex-partner loves their children and wants the best for them as you do, and it's comforting to know that someone else is there for your children too, it's not just you
- If your ex-partner is still present, then they are there to help, if you are sick or you have work commitments
- They can be a voice of reason, seeing things with a fresh perspective.

You and the Dad or the Mum

If their father/mother is still around, it is worth while trying your best to make a friend out of your ex, for the sake of your children and for you too. In a way it honours what you once had, though it isn't always easy. Adjusting to a new way of life can initially be uncharted waters and it's easy to get caught up in frustrations, seemingly caused by the absent parent. You will find yourself needing to vent your frustrations. The big rule is to not disrespect your children's mother or father in front of them. They get confused about their loyalties and can feel guilty about loving their mum or dad, if they feel that it is going to upset you. If your children ask why you separated, spare them from the gritty raw emotions and details. Speak calmly and factually about what went on. Children are smart and can draw their own conclusions as to who acted unfairly. If you need to vent about your ex, then do it with friends, a counsellor or simply write it out of you.

Why do some Dads and Mums Abscond?

Some parents feel overwhelmed by the responsibility of the commitment in raising a child. When a child comes along your life changes – it has to. From selfish you become selfless and your life revolves around that child, because their survival depends on that. Some men find it hard to deal with. Your attention is no longer centred on them, whilst others can't get to grips with the material needs a father should contribute to the family. There are also physiological reasons – maybe they feel that they would fail and be a disappointment to you and the child, so it's therefore easier to run away. Becoming a parent is a big step and some simply are just not ready to take it, so they abscond. Children aren't always planned and it maybe that the mother isn't the father's choice for a committed relationship. There are many reasons, yet it all comes down to failing to be able to take responsibility of the life they helped create. It's not just fathers, there are mothers too who cannot deal with parenthood and leave the father holding the child.

My Situation

My daughter's father is no longer living in the same country as us and he has very little to do with us. There are occasional phone calls.

To my daughter, he is a voice at the other end of a phone line, who she doesn't really understand. He left when she was 19-months-old after a series of violent outbursts, leaving her with a completely broken mum. He has never returned to the UK. I have been unsure of the welcome we would receive if we travelled to visit him alone. I have tried to keep a flow of communication going, but with constant changing numbers and no long-term residence, it's been hard. I have explained to my daughter that her dad is a bit nomadic, it's his nature to wander. The reason that he isn't present and calling, or sending gifts, isn't because of anything that she has done. I find this quite challenging to write, because I wish my daughter had a dad who was responsive to her. She deserves that, every child deserves that. And in my heart I can only have faith that one day my daughter and her dad do have some sort of relationship, to give her peace of mind, if nothing else.

No Access

The only time that I would advise you to deny access or unsupervised access to the mother or father is if they are abusive, suffer from substance abuse, the environment where they are hosting your child is questionable or you feel that they may take the children away from you. You have to make that judgement and in your heart you will know the right call to make.

Your Children's Reaction to Life without Dad

How your child may react to parental separation varies in the different age groups. By recognising the signs, you will be able to offer your child extra support. It's so important that you keep the flow of communication open, so that your children know what's going on. Do spare them from the nitty-gritty, just make them aware of imminent change to their lives. It's important if dad or mum is still around so that they also communicate with them regularly. Encourage your children to speak honestly to you. It sometimes takes a while for them to be able to articulate how they are feeling. Let them legitimise their feelings before you offer ways to make it better.

Consistency is so important for young children. Keep the routine visits with dad regular if possible. Ask them if they are happy with the routine, the scheduled days with dad. It may be that a teenager doesn't want to be shipped off to them for the weekends when they are at age where their social calendar is of the utmost importance. Your child didn't ask for his or her parents to separate, so it is important that they are happy with the new schedule.

Infants and Toddlers

At this age, routine is of paramount importance, it's how they feel safe. When that routine changes there may be excessive crying, digestive problems, change to their regular sleep and eating habits. Toddlers may become increasingly lethargic, there may be an increase in temper tantrums, night terrors and a regression into previous younger patterns.

Two to three-year-olds

For this age group, dealing with separation from a parent may cause heightened irritability, aggression, temper tantrums, regression, a loss of recently acquired skills and a heightened reaction to separation from either parent.

Three to seven-year-olds

They have a limited ability to make sense of parental loss. This may lead them to feel that it is something that they have done and the loss is their fault in some way. There may be a regression in the loss of developmental accomplishments – language, motor activities, or emotional independence, a change to sleep and eating patterns, or excessive clinging to either parent. At school they may appear anxious, be restless, moody, and show signs of stress and depression. Their school work may regress, showing less initiative or willingness to participate. They may be withdrawn or become very sensitive and reactive with their peers. They may complain of physical symptoms such as headaches, stomach problems, extreme tiredness, this is the child's unconscious attempt to have increased contact with you the parent. Parental welfare and the idea of remarriage are a large concern to this age group.

Eight to 12-year olds

They are aware of what is going on and they will feel divided over loyalties. Their emotions of sadness and helplessness may be expressed through anger. It will be easier for them to express through anger, rather than to open up their emotional vulnerability. They may show signs of low self-esteem and decreased academic performance.

Teenagers

Teenagers are already going through massive changes, as they transition from child to teenager. They are already dealing with their emerging sexual feelings, forging their own identity in the world and desiring more independence. Separating parents is an added stress to the changes that they are already experiencing. They will need emotional support, acceptance, love and guidance from both their parents. As teenagers, there are new ways that they may express their distress. These could be recreational drugs, physical damage, reckless actions as well as showing signs of low self-esteem. They may suffer from depression, insomnia, hypersomnia, poor concentration, low energy, fatigue, feelings of hopelessness and feel withdrawn from friends and family. Dealing with parents dating and remarriage is also challenging and it can all seem confusing to them, as they have their loyalties to their parent.

My daughter went through a difficult time. When she was overcome with emotions of being rejected and abandoned by her father, these emotions surfaced four years after her father left. She was angry and would often get physical and become very destructive. This wasn't her normal behaviour, so I knew that it was a phase that she was needing to process. Knowing this allowed me to let her do what she needed to do, without reprimanding her. Instead I encouraged her to draw her feelings out with aggressive scribbling or to dance to a fast beat track, to dispel some of the pent-up emotions. After we sit down and let it go, if she wants to talk about anything then I offer the ear, the love and the explanations that will pacify her.

Be aware of how your child is reacting to the changes. Offer them warmth, love and emotional support. Keep enforcing age-related discipline and realistic boundaries. Contact from both parents is very important for their wellbeing, so that they know that they aren't disappearing from their lives. It's a sad time for all and you can really comfort each other by sharing and looking positively to the future.

CHAPTER 14

Peaceful Parenting

For a Peaceful Life, with your Peaceful Children

Inner peace is great. It's a sign of tranquillity and being unaffected by negative disturbances.

Raising children with peace and teaching them ways to achieve inner peace too, is to everyone's advantage.

During relationship breakdowns, the home environment can be anything but peaceful. It can feel like a stress-filled hothouse and then a sad house to you and your little people. These emotions are past, so there is no point in rehashing memories to feel guilty. Boom – past is gone! Now is the time to concentrate on creating a peaceful home for your children. When there is peace there is happy energy present. We can be relaxed and centred in the way we parent when there is peace within. Creating a peaceful home life for you and your children to thrive in is paramount to all your successes and a lot of the process of creating peace is how we parent and how we choose to react.

Hints to getting that peaceful vibe flowing

Understand the true value of peace. If there is a constant surge of noise from computer games, banging musical beats, excitable play and dramatic TV shows endlessly blaring through your home it becomes difficult for your mind to rest, as it's constantly being stimulated by external factors. This is also true for your children. We all need quiet time to digest new learnings and process daily events. Peace allows us to also be creative.

Introduce a 'Quiet Time' into your day, after mealtime is a good time as it allows you to digest your food efficiently too. Just relax. Read, sit in the garden, have cuddle time, just take some time out of your busyness to just be. Being able to be relaxed and silent in someone else's company isn't a bad thing. Lead by example. Children do tend to model their behaviour on the way we behave. They use our language, mannerisms, body language etc. It's often quite scary to see someone so small mirror your lesser side back to you, or in role play game with their friends. Be balanced and diplomatic, whilst dealing with frustrations in front of your children. Then they will subconsciously absorb that behaviour into their psyche and project it into their interactions with people throughout their life.

Do everything in moderation – a great lesson. Find your personal balance and know your limits. They are good bench marks to find. By doing so you are aware of the results of overburdening yourself, the frazzled nerves and general irritation. You can explain to your child the benefits of moderation and help them to find that place within themselves.

Live simply. Too many complications can result in unnecessary stress. Too much stuff creates too much stuff to clean up, speaking both metaphorically and actually. Limit your commitments so that you don't feel like you are endlessly chasing your tail and ferrying your children around to different activities. Social events are part of the parenting journey, yet maybe have one day a week which you keep free.

Be proactive where it allows. If and when problems arise deal with them sooner rather than later. Nip it in the bud, so that peace can again be restored.

Teaching good sportsmanship and its importance. Bringing our children up to value fairness is really important. It's great to be a winner, but it's not all or nothing. Trying our best and working towards the best that we can be is important. Understanding good sportsmanship gives them a great chance of growing up to value egalitarianism in all forms.

Acting without expectations. Expectations in a way can stop

the natural flow towards the natural outcome. If we enter situations with high expectations then we are almost setting ourselves up for disappointment. Take part in activities for the sheer fun of it, rather than focusing on unrealistic expectations with your children and yourself.

Know how and when to discipline. Children will break house rules and social rules constantly. It is part of their journey to test boundaries. As parents, we must learn to recognise their behaviour. For example, is it out of plain naughtiness and the need for attention, or is it them simply growing up? If it is them growing up, then it is time to adjust the rules/boundaries. Talking calmly to them and coming up with a solution to the problem will pay off. Be flexible, so that you are both ultimately happy.

If you are having an off-day and your children are pushing every button they can, walk away, until the inner Zen has returned. I used to sit in my car and listen to the radio for 10 minutes, until I was in a different head space and the 'I am going to lose it' feeling had passed. Losing your temper with your kids isn't cool, because we say and do things that can be very damaging. At the end of the day, kids are kids. You have to be responsible for your reactions. Discipline your child by giving them extra chores or removing some privileges and communicating to them about why their behaviour was out of line.

Reacting to your Child's Outburst and Misbehaviours

Children have a lot to deal in their life and when their parents are separating and their world is being turned upside, they don't always know how to articulate strong emotions. These may just surface in an angry outburst or misbehaviour. You know your child better than anyone and you know if they are behaving out of character. Firstly, don't react, let the outburst pass and take nothing personally. When everything has become calmer, gently talk to your child. Help them to open up and then help them to see things from a fresh perspective. Part of the passage of being a parent is helping to shine the light of clarity onto your children's dramas in a calm, peaceful and non-judgemental way. Communication is key in every relationship and by being able to communicate efficiently to your children, they will then do the same in their friendships and relationships, because they have had a great teacher.

You, Your Kids and Rules

Raising a child or children alone often has many challenges. Disciplining a child when you are by yourself can be testing. Being 'good cop, bad cop' can send out mixed messages. Personally, I can find it very draining being the sole authoritarian to my daughter, for many reasons. There is no one in my corner giving back-up to the house rules. I also feel for my daughter, as she doesn't have an ally. I also don't enjoy listening to the sound of my repetitive nags any more than my daughter does. It can be tiring being the continual law enforcer, especially during the boundary testing phases, of which there are many. I personally choose to bring my daughter up by disciplining with peaceful assertiveness. I don't believe that there is any need for smacking or over-the-top punishments for bad behaviour.

Communication is the key, so that there can be understanding. Bad behaviour isn't only a result of naughtiness, it can be the child's way of expressing pent-up emotions that they are too young to know how to express. Naughtiness often comes and goes in phases, can be a result of tiredness, stress, may arise from feeling insecure, being upset with world, being confused or it can also be for attention.

Trying behaviour can be a challenge to deal with. It's draining. Children know exactly how to press our buttons to get a reaction and it can take a lot of our own inner willpower not to react negatively. There is a lot to be said about deep breathing. When you feel the red haze from within rising, take time out. My own daughter isn't always angelic – she is very strong-willed and we often clash, sometimes even head on. In these moments the only solution is 'time out'. I sit outside or in the car, so that I can recompose myself, to deal with the aftermath calmly. I don't ever want to crush my daughter spirit, because she needs her strength to serve her well in her life. When we are both composed, we talk about what it was we clashed over. I explain things from my perspective so that she may understand where I am coming from, and I listen to her feelings. If you are co-parenting, it is advisable to have the same 'house rules', though this often isn't the case. This will encourage continuity and your children won't feel confused, or view one parent as good cop and the other as bad cop.

Some Effective Guidelines

Communication is key

Clearly outline the type of behaviour that you deem acceptable and outline clearly what is not acceptable. Explain why. Be sure to back yourself up, there is no point in having a code of law and order if you don't stay true to your word. Staying true to our words gives the words added power. Communicating about bad behaviour will also give you a clear insight as to where your child is emotionally. From there you can determine the root cause and then appropriate action to resolve any problems. Your child may just need a big hug after having a shocking day at school.

Review the house rules

As children grow up and become responsible, the rules need to adapt to their new levels of maturity. Often children will fight against boundaries when they feel that they have out grown them. Trusting that your child will do the right thing gives them confidence to do the right thing, as there is nothing to rebel against.

Praise good behaviour

Giving praise, gratitude and acknowledging good actions, however small, has an overall positive effect. Children love and crave parental approval. Praise builds up their confidence and it's a positive affirmation for them to receive, to confirm that their efforts have not gone unnoticed. Focusing on the good behaviour can also reduce bad behaviour.

Ignore Misbehaviour

Bad behaviour can be sometimes be for attention and showing off. If it is the case, ignoring them until they begin to behave in a way that you deem acceptable. If your child is speaking to you in a whinny or demanding tone, tell them that you won't hear a word they are saying until they speak normally. It may take a while, but their need for your attention will revert them back to speaking normally once again.

Time Out

This is an effective disciplining strategy. It gives everyone some space and time to calm down and reflect. Choose a designated spot in your home, a chair for example. Mentally mark it the 'chair of tranquillity', rather than labelling it the 'naughty step'. You want your child to go there to calm down. During this time out (as a rule of thumb it is usually one minute for every year of their life), refrain from engaging in conversation with them. This is their alone time, for working out what they did wrong and why. After the time has elapsed, discuss it. Children can be remorseful. It's important that you acknowledge it, hug and move on.

Behaviour Chart

A chart can highlight to your child all the things that they are doing well and routinely. There is no need for it to be a reward motivated chart. A good dose of encouraging praise and a sticker should be enough. We all like to receive praise and acknowledgement for things that we have made an effort in, children even more so.

Boss Voice

Make sure that you have an "I am the BOSS" tone to your voice. Being able to change the pitch to your voice can be a real indicator to your children that they are getting close to the edge or that what you are saying really needs to be taken on-board. Yelling and screeching at them only teaches them to zone out to you, or learn that shouting is an acceptable way of communicating, which of course it isn't.

Redirection

Redirect your child's attention to something that you feel happier with them doing. This works well for siblings. If one is disturbing the other's peaceful play, redirect the annoying one to something that will divert their attention away from bothering their sibling. With siblings, it is important to see them as individuals. The older one needs to have greater freedom, whilst the younger one has to understand that when they are that age they too will receive the same freedom. This will give the older child the sense that they are trusted and the younger one something to aspire to.

Consequences

Teaching your children that there are consequences to misbehaving is an important part of discipline. A resulting consequence can be a removal of a privileges, or a favoured possession being confiscated. It can be very effective and works equally well for teenagers. You know your child's favoured attachments and you should use this to your advantage.

Intervention

Occasionally external help is needed. If you are experiencing a naughty phase which seems to be ongoing and you feel at your wits end (because it happens) ask someone who has both yours and your child's best interests at heart to intervene. Just by someone having a gentle chat to your child, they may be able to find out what's going on. Often we are too attached to the problem. The child shouldn't feel that they are being ganged up upon and it should be a done primarily out of concern.

CHAPTER 15

Many Hands Make Light Work

Chores

Sharing the load of domestic chores can really work to your advantage, so that you feel you have a little bit of help at home, which can be a huge relief. When my daughter does something thoughtful at home, however small the action maybe, it just sends me over the moon. I am not trying to encourage and advocate free child labour, or overburdening your child with unnecessary adult responsibility. But teaching children to take some responsibility and to cultivate a helpful demeanour, apart from assisting you presently, will serve them well in their future life.

Generally speaking, children like to help. Young kids like to play at being mum, they like to watch you and mimic your actions. My daughter was very small when she donned the marigolds and sprayed cleaning spray everywhere. Obviously, I filled the bottle with water to avoid accidents, but she loved it as it was play. Sadly, at the young age, with overwhelming enthusiasm her efforts were more play mess orientated than actually helpful. It was a joy to watch her, but sadly nothing was really achieved.

Domestic chores need to be handed out responsibly so that the child is doing something that is age skill related, so that a good result can be attained from their efforts. You know your child and their capabilities better than anyone else, so even though I have included lists below, use your own judgement on your child's capabilities. It's important to praise your child for a job well done, so they feel appreciated and are happy to continue helping. It's also good for their confidence and personal development.

Making chore time fun

Rewards can be given if this is something you agree with, for a job well done. Pocket money can be earned when the jobs have been done. You can do a little potluck challenge - pick chores out of top hat or a clowns hat, and then grade the end result, always give generous marks as a way to encourage your children's enthusiasm, and then just give them a few handy hints so they can improve.

Remember the more help you get at home, the more time you have outside the house to enjoy cycle rides, shopping trips and play days out.

You can involve your children in your weekly grocery shopping. This will help them to understand healthy dietary choices and shopping within a budget. You can encourage them to help out in the kitchen. These are all great life skills that you are imparting to your children. Chores are life skills. They are good habits to have instilled, as they aren't always going to be living at home. I have had many flatmates and you can tell those whom have an inbuilt clean gene, to those whom are just plain slothful and expect someone else to wash the dishes, clean the bathroom, change the loo paper etc. In the long-term they aren't fun to live with. I would advise that if you have more than one child, to spread the duties equally. The last thing you want to do is create friction between your children, if one has a long old list and the other does a lot less. Get them to work as a happy little team.

Suggested chores for five to seven-year-olds

Sweeping floors
Bed-making
Tidying their bedrooms
Tidying up after making some mess

Feeding the pets
Setting the table
Helping to clear the dishes
Hanging up towels after washing
Putting dirty clothes in the laundry basket

Suggested chores for eight to 10-year-olds

Loading the dishwasher
Putting away the groceries
Making their own breakfast
Hanging out the laundry
Helping in the garden
Helping prepare dinner
Dusting
Packing their own sports kits

Suggested chores for 11 to 15-year-olds

Vacuuming
Washing the floor
Washing windows
Using the washing machine
Walking the dog
Cleaning the bathroom

CHAPTER 16

What Kids Love

Kids love fun. However you have to provide fun for children, it's their golden pass to happyville. Our children's simplicity is a gentle reminder to ourselves to stop, take a check of our serious levels and rebalance them with play. Life is too flipping short to get stuck in serious stress mode all the time. Why would you not want to experience fun, adventure and freedom with your children? Reclaim your inner child, remembering a time when you to held the innocence of play, before the heartbreaks, the bills, the responsibilities and the career ladders to climb.

Kids love hanging out with their parents, but they too love the company of other children. Going on adventures with friends and their kids is a great way for you to joint socialise. Activities don't need to cost an arm and a leg. They just need to be entertaining.

List of Fun Kids Activities

Foraging

Foraging can make any walk in the country fun, educational and an adventure. There is so many edible goodies to forage in the UK, especially in the spring, summer and early autumn months.

Spring – wild garlic leaves, dandelions, nettles, sorrel, hops
Summer – blackberries, brambles, raspberries, mulberries, wild

rose petals, edible flowers, elder flowers, black currants, wild strawberries, oregano, mint, wild herbs, damsons, elderberries, plums

Autumn – apples, pears, crab apples, sloes, chestnuts

Certain mushrooms are available all year round. However, pick with someone who has expert mushroom knowledge – eating the wrong mushroom, or a toadstool, can be fatal. To identify leaves, herbs, berries, fruits and flowers that can be foraged refer to a book if you are unsure. With your edible treasures, you can transform them into tasty meals. Refer to recipes. Whilst out on your walk, you can collect wild flowers that can be pressed. After the pressing process, they can be transformed into artistic masterpieces – book marks, cards, pictures, collages.

Gardening

Getting kids interested in garden life is so educational. They love being outdoors, playing, making dens, jumping on the trampoline, making potions, playing with a bat and ball, chalking on pavements, skipping, kicking a football around, sprinkler fun – it's an endless list. Apart from all the play, encourage them to help in the garden and grow their own plants, vegetables, herbs and flowers. If you have no outdoor space, then plant in tubs. Get birdfeeders, either in your garden or the ones that suck themselves to your windows, and start teaching them the birds' names. You can make your own bee home, to attract bees into your outdoor space. Promote garden time.

Camping

Camping is cheap and something different from the normal day to day. Campsites are often filled with families, so you and your children get to socialise and make holiday buddies – look up family-friendly sites. Cooking over a little camping stove, sleeping in the rain, toasting marshmallows, stargazing, being outside until twilight and running around with freedom makes the camping adventure magical for kids.

You can get some great deals on basic camping kits or borrow from a friend. I suggest going for a couple of nights initially. If it's not your thing, you have the comfort of knowing that you will soon be home. If you do like it you can go for longer the next time.

Creative Play

Allow your kids to be creative. You can structure their creative pursuits with a few basic rules, so that you don't end up with a glittery-sticky home. Keep an art drawer filled with old boxes, paints, old wrapping paper, old cards, glue, sparkling things, etc. It will give them hours of fun. Find out new creative things to do at home. It's ideal for wet days. You can then decorate the house with their latest masterpieces. You can always join in the fun and create some fabulous one-off masterpieces too.

Sports

It's all too easy to stay in and watch rerun after rerun of kiddie drama, or let the kids get absorbed in computer games for hours on end – sometimes even days. Encouraging sports or sport activities is beneficial to everyone's wellbeing. Sport helps to release pent-up frustrations. It also helps to keep children physically and mentally healthy. Sport aids self-esteem issues. Let your child lead you to the sports that they love. They can try many sports, but they may not necessarily want to commit to a season and you want to be faced with resistance every time that it's time for class. Taking your children to classes is a good way for you too to meet other parents and get connected to the local community.

Being part of a team dynamic is a great lesson for 'working together'. Partaking in healthy competitions is a valuable lesson in learning good sportsmanship and learning to win and lose gracefully. If your child has a natural talent for a sport, encouraging that to grow may really help to open doors for them in the future. It's positive for your children to see you enjoying sport too.

Spontaneous Day Trips

There is nothing like jumping in the car and ending up somewhere totally unplanned. If it's a day trip to the seaside, a country picnic, a night away or a fun park excursion, spontaneous days are smashing surprises. Seeing your child's face light up at the idea of a joyful surprise is priceless.

Spontaneous Gifts

Well really, who doesn't love a surprise gift? Birthdays and Christmas can feel like eons to wait when you are little. Sometimes I buy my daughter a little gift, hide it under her pillow or at the foot of the bed or just treasure seek it out. It's so much fun and because it's a surprise and there is no expectation. It's generally received with real gratitude.

Culture Made Fun

Check in with your children to see what they are studying at school and find museums and exhibitions that correspond. Ask them to teach you, play dumb – it helps them articulate what they have learnt and it's role-reversal. It's great for their confidence. You can always discover new pearls of wisdom together. There are so many wonderful interactive museums and they are often free entry.

Cooking

At a young age, cooking is play. Concocting weird and wonderful shades of icing is all part of the game. It's a life lesson. There are days when you are in a rush and the last thing you want is lots of busy little people under your feet, whilst trying to get dinner on the table. When you do have time, invest it in teaching them. When they get older they can really become involved in the meal preparations.

Dancing

Let them take charge of the stereo and let them shake their thing to their favourite tunes. It's very entertaining. Bodies love to move and no more so than little bodies – encouraging dance to be spontaneous just helps the rhythm of life to flow. I don't know anyone who doesn't feel better for a boogie and you too can get involved.

Festivals

Festivals aren't every one's cup of tea. Over recent years, festivals have become increasingly popular and there are now many festivals that are really geared towards families. It is a wonderful way to spend a weekend doing something different. There are many activities and workshops on offer. Being outside in a very relaxed environment, children meet other kids and they just have the freedom to roam. There is a growth in the number of festivals that are alcohol and drug-free zones. The folks at these festivals are generally high on life or wheatgrass shots. Festivals are social, giving you the opportunity to mingle and meet new people too.

Conscious parties

Who doesn't love to party? Organised conscious parties are alcohol and drug-free dance environments, suitable for families – if you love a boogie, why not?

New Places

Explore new places, whether it's overseas or just roaming closer to home. There is so much to see, we really live in a multicultural society presently and its great getting out and about, trying new cuisine, experiencing different religious festivals and understanding the different cultures that make up this world.

Chilling Out

Children have busy lives and often they just want to chill out. Just having a quiet day at home can be perfect.

Movie Nights

For regular family movie nights get the popcorn popping, the blankets out, the chill-out clothes on and cuddle up on the sofa and watch comedies or age-appropriate films together.

Freedom

This applies to older children. It's important to your child to let them know you trust them. Giving them some freedom helps them to take some responsibility. Obviously, the level of freedom you give a child should be age-appropriate, as well as suiting the level of maturity your child has. You also need to feel comfortable.

Mum and Dad

Most of all kids love their mum and dad, whatever the external appearances are. They may test your boundaries, they may vent their frustrations and teenagers rebel – it's just part of them growing up. If they couldn't do it with you, who would they do it too? They love you, in your child's world you are the most important person to them. Never forget that. Take as much time as you can to hang out with them. It has such a positive effect and really helps you to know and understand their development, and forms a wonderful grounded relationship.

Balancing children's emotions with Flower and Gem Essences

Growing up is full of pressures, both external and from within and children often don't know how to balance their emotions. Balancing emotions is something you learn from experience. Young ones can become overwhelmed with new strong feelings that they have previously not had to deal with.

A small playground incident can feel like a huge drama to a child, who can retreat within. When their parents are separating and their world as they knew it is being destroyed, they can often feel deeply unsettled.

Some children take on the responsibility of the separation, others may rebel and feel very angry and confused. Some children are carrying the scars of sadness from watching their parents rip each other apart for a period of time. Children go through a lot and it is often good to have something on hand to soothe their mind and emotions.

Flower and crystal essences are a form of energy healing. Their calming energies help to rebalance and restore the feeling of inner centred connection once again. They are completely natural and don't cause adverse side effects. It is possible to experience a greater degree of tiredness and transient mood changes, as the energy matrix of the essence is working on the blocked emotions. I have gone into more detail about 'what is a flower essence' on page 66.

I have been drawn toward the Indigo Essence range which I use for my own daughter. This range of gem essences was created by Ann Callaghan with the help of her nephews. Ann created this range after years of listening to children telling her what bothered them. Ann is an Irish homoeopath and began to use them in her practice, to assist children and their families deal with their problems. There are many individual essences under the Indigo umbrella, yet I will be focusing on the combination essence range, which is a collection of 12 essences and it is an emotional rescue kit for children and their parents.

Champion

This essence combination helps the child who is timid and afraid of others. They may get picked on and be hesitant and afraid. This remedy will help the child to find his or her inner strength.

Chill

This help when a child feels very angry and can't seem to find a way out of it. It's normal to get angry now and again, but sometimes you can get stuck in the anger and this is where chill can help. It will help you talk about what is making you angry and how to resolve it.

Confidence

Helps the child that lacks self-confidence and is filled with self-doubt. It helps the child to feel that they are special and extraordinary just the way they are and that there is nothing to prove to anyone.

Happy

This is for when children are feeling sad a lot and don't know why. It is also for children whom hide their sadness and pretend that everything is okay, they may believe that if they start crying they will never stop. Happy wants the child to know and be reassured that it is ok to cry. The tears will come to an end and happiness will shine once again.

Invisible Friend

For when a child feels that they have no friends and that they are all on their own. It will help the child to feel that there is love and support for them.

Love

Love is for times when a child feels that no one loves them.

No Fear

This is for children who are sensitive and timid, who easily feel afraid. This helps to give them a feeling of protection and courage. It helps them to understand that everyone feels scared sometimes and that they are not alone. You will always be loved and looked after by your guardian angel.

Plurk

For a child who gets stressed easily and may take life too seriously – they feel they need to succeed and achieve and that life is a serious business. Plurk encourages the feelings of fun.

Settle

This essence is for a child who feels terribly uncomfortable in their physical body and cannot focus their attention on anything for too long. Settle encourages them to relax and to know that it is safe just to be.

Shine

For a child whom has learnt to act with coldness, cynicism and unfeeling so that they may fit into their peer group, this remedy helps you to know that it is safe to be who you really are, so that you can help other kids to be who they really are.

Sleep Easy

This helps the child who feels spooked at night, often when children are very sensitive to energies and find it hard to relax enough to go to sleep.

The Works

This essence helps you to remember the point of it all and will help your child to carry on with their life. The works is for children who are feeling lost. The works wants them to know that they are much loved and all the help you need is just working for you. Works can be used in an emergency, like a rescue remedy – it will help to stabilise the energy body. The works can work particularly well on the older teenager, who is flipping out and close to doing damage to themselves.

These are concentrated essences and can be diluted by adding a few drops to a glass of water or alternatively adding a few drops to a plain moisturiser and rub it into the skin. They are also available in room sprays.

CHAPTER 17

Home Is Where The Heart Is

The marital home often becomes another victim of the divorce settlement and selling your home becomes the only viable option available. The sale of your house often means that you may have to downsize to a more affordable compromise.

The initial change isn't always greeted favourably. Your children may have friends close by, you too may have a core of supportive and friendly neighbours. Your daily routine and the pattern to your life is often strongly connected to your home. It too is another new beginning and another realisation to the fact that your separation is finalising and you are entering the unfamiliar world of lone parenting.

It's not always easy making the change. You may visit many potential new properties before you walk into the one that you feel has the promise of being a good home to you and your children. Children are adaptable, we are all adaptable and when you are surrounded with the things that you love, your new house becomes your home. My daughter has taught me this time and time again. We live in a one bedroom maisonette – it's small, I yearn for my own bedroom with a bed, a garden, more space. She does too, yet at the end of an active day at work and school we walk through the door to familiarity, to the place we call home, where we relax and kick back. It's warm, its cosy (maybe a bit too), it's clean, it's safe and it's affordable to run and live in.

When choosing your new home, be realistic. Work out your budget to include everything – the utilities, the council tax, insurance and commuting costs for your daily essential trips. Don't put more pressure on yourself than is necessary. If you are renting, then you can always move again once you feel more established financially.

Moving into a new dwelling can offer you a chance to put your stamp on your new home. Decorate how you wish so that you feel comfortable. It's great to let your children be creative with their new sleeping space too. You can treat it as a family project. It's a positive way to move forward and welcome in the change.

You can get generous friends to teach and help you with DIY. Most people that I have asked have been sympathetic to my situation and are willing to help, for love or a small fee. They have always happily helped, putting up the odd shelf, hang blinds, fixing the loo, helping with the little things. It's a rewarding feeling letting someone help. If you can, try to learn as many little DIY skills from them, so that in the future you can attempt it yourself. In the future, I can have the confidence to put up the shelves and do the basics.

Remember that 'One man's trash can be another man's gold'. If you are on a tight budget, there are auction sites – eBay, Gumtree – and 'freecycle' schemes. Wander through car boot sales, charity shops, second-hand shops, antique shops and fairs, markets and discount bins in department stores. By searching in the right places, you can find some real treasures, whether you are looking for fabrics, beds, three-piece lounge suite, or table and chairs, you can find some inexpensive items that can add lot of character and individuality to your home.

It's important to determine the look and style that you are going for. Whether you are striving towards a classic country feel, urban warehouse vibe, vintage chic, bohemian Moroccan, fifties, sixties or seventies retro, or whether you are after modern minimalism. If you are feeling a bit clueless, do some research. Flick through the pages of glossy magazines for creative inspiration.

For creating a peaceful and harmonious space you can consider the eastern philosophies of Feng Shui and Vaastu. These are both ancient teachings from China and India retrospectively. They are the knowledge that reveals how to balance the energy in the space to assure health and good fortune to all the people that are inhabiting it. Both Feng Shui and Vaastu work by balancing the five elements – earth, air, sky, water and fire. These are represented by north, south, east and west compass points. The correct placement of objects can encourage good fortune and harmony into your space. Both philosophies can be used if you wish, when making structural changes to your property. There is a lot to explore in both teachings.

Your new house can become the home that you have always wanted to create. Unleash your inner creative spirit and really enjoy putting your new home together. Learn your way around a sewing machine, even if you have had no prior experience, you can pick it up pretty quickly and create some wonderful works. The internet is a wonderful haven for teaching tutorials. You can learn how to upcycle old furniture, how to restore classic pieces, how to make curtains – the creative list is endless.

Once you are settled into your new abode, keeping your home in a good order is so important for you and your children's wellbeing. Home needs to be a sanctuary, where you retreat to after a busy day, a place where you can relax and rejuvenate, feel cosy, warm and safe.

Tips for keeping and making a home homely

Clean as you go along
Have a mental or visual cleaning rota to help stay on top of things
Do seasonal 'spring cleans', hire in help if you need it
Keep the glass in your windows clean
Get rid of anything that doesn't make you feel happy (or hide it)
Keep organised, encourage your children to put things where they
    should go
Open all the windows once a day, to circulate your home with fresh air
Open all the curtains and blinds to let in the natural light
Stay on top of the DIY, get broken things fixed or get rid
Light candles, the flame helps to create the visual warmth in your home
Have fresh cut flowers
Plants in your home can really improve the atmosphere as they are
    natural air purifiers and oxygen generators (suggestions include
    peace lily, aloe vera, philodendron, snake plant to name a few)

If you have a garden keep it so that it's manageable

Scent your home, either with candles, natural diffusers, oil burners or incense

Declutter and detox your home

Clear the energetic space of your home regularly

Create an inspiration or 'wish board' of places that you and your children want to visit, or things that you want to create in your life, goals that you want to achieve

Fill your home with things that bring happiness

Have small joyous social gatherings for your children and their friends, and for you and your friends

Have a creative wall to display all your children's masterpieces.

CHAPTER 18

Green Living

Go Organic

O rganically grown food has a higher nutritional value. Organic produce has to be farmed without the use of harmful chemicals, fertilizers and pesticides, synthetic hormones or antibiotics. The soil is certified organic and the foods are free from GM (genetically modified) ingredients. Organic produce offers a win-win solution for your health. Pesticides and chemical sprays have been linked to causing weakness and imbalances within the immune system and the nervous system, so it is highly advisable to avoid foods that have been sprayed. If you find your supermarket's choice a bit limiting or expensive, you may try growing your own vegetables or visiting pick-your-own farms. There are also many companies that deliver boxes of seasonal freshly picked organic goodies to your door, and farmers' markets attract many local farm sellers.

Eating Organic

Much of the food that we buy is sprayed with a cocktail of pesticides. In the long-term these aren't good for our health. Fruit, vegetables and animal products that have been farmed in traditional and natural ways are so much better for you, as well as for the environment. Much of the soil that has been used for mass and continuous farming is very depleted of nutrients. Thus, the vegetables that are grown on such land are also depleted in vitamins and nutrients that our bodies require for optimum health. If we demand food that hasn't been sprayed with chemical fertilizers and pesticides, surely more natural ways will have to be used in food production. As consumers, we have great power, as it is our hard-earned pennies that are funding these multinational powerhouse companies. Rather than getting swept up in the subliminal messages fed to us through clever advertising, we can start taking back our consumer power and demanding the best. Food that is produced, reared and grown locally is world friendly.

Eco Living

Eco Living is all about respecting the world we live in. At the moment our world is drowning in waste and is being suffocated by personal and industrial pollution. We are exhausting the natural resources that supply us with everyday fuel necessities. Global warming isn't just going to disappear overnight if we don't talk about it. In our lifetime, we continually witness the strange weather patterns, as the natural status quo of the world is certainly out of sync. We as individuals need to start to take responsibility for what we do and how we behave towards the earth. When our children see us integrating recycling, composting, reusing, not being wasteful and using energy efficient methods in our everyday life, it will be a natural way for them to behave in the same way in the future. As parents, it's part of our parenting responsibility to educate our children in living in harmony with the earth. As hippy as that may sound, it's not. It's wisdom from the ancients, which has been suppressed by the material industrialised age that we are currently living in.

Being green, being Eco, is cool. It's the new black or maybe the new rainbow! If you know that you are doing something positive to reduce your carbon footprint, the knock-on effect is that you feel positive. Living green doesn't just benefit the planet, it also helps you and your children to remain healthy. There are so many chemicals in our everyday products that we are unaware of. In small doses they don't cause harm, yet combined over time, they build up as toxicity in our bodies and this can lead to allergies, illness and other serious ailments.

Making a positive change towards living a greener life is first about identifying the grey areas in your lifestyle. Do you drive unnecessarily, do you buy food that is flown half way around the world before it reaches your plate, do you buy magazines, papers etc and don't read them? How much junk mail comes unwittingly through your letter box? Take a look at your heating habits and your electricity dependency. How many light bulbs are on at one time in your home, how many standby lights are on, how much waste are you generating every week, every year? What's in the products that you are buying, how are they being produced? Water is another bill we pay for, so look at the water flowing into and out of your home.

You may well be feeling overwhelmed about this topic so far. You may choose to ignore it, because you aren't in the right head space to make the changes and that's fine temporarily. If you can and are willing, take small steps to make positive changes to your life style, because it's the small steps that we take that make up the distance. If you are super keen and ready for big environmental changes to the way you live, do research. I am just opening the door here, to a glowing green world of possibilities and I am just touching the surface of what's out there.

Green Fingers

'Growing your own' is chic. If there is a desire to grow your own, then a way will present itself. Growing your own is no longer something that is an exclusive pursuit for the retired, or those with colossal back yards. It's a pastime available to all. If you have no garden space you become an urban grower, use pots, grow bags, hanging baskets and kitchen window sills. You can enquire with your local council about available allotment space. Allotments are great, but as with most things in life you get out of it what you put in, so they can be time-consuming. However, if you like the idea of an allotment with an abundance of edible goodies, maybe share the space with a friend. Many hands make light work and of course it's great for companionship. If your friend has children too, you can assign a piece of the allotment land to all the children. Then they can be really involved and included in the 'grow your own' project. You can advise them on what to do, give them the skills and then let them get on with it. It's a great way for them to learn about growing fresh produce, to delegate the work, to take responsibility within the team and to problem solve to come up with practical solutions.

Growing your own has much going for it. It's seasonal, organic, it's cheap, it has no carbon footprint, there is no plastic packaging, it's the freshest way of eating you can imagine. Everything is loaded with nutrients, vitamins and life-giving force. As well as the nutritional and global plus points, it's a fun and practical way to teach your children about nature and where food really comes from. I bet they will eat their home-grown vegetables and fruits, because they have witnessed the amazing transformation from seed to edible delight. Growing your own teaches your children patience, which is a much-needed lesson, as the world is so fast that we are almost programmed to believe that everything should be instantaneous.

Once you start growing your own and are aware of the work and effort involved, there becomes a new level of respect for food, something that is lacking in much of the developed world. I believe this to be mainly due to the cultural popularity of supermarkets and their endless food supplies. Food is just picked off the shelves. Very little thought goes into where it came from, how it was grown, how it got there – it's popped into the trolley and either eaten or thrown out when the sell by date tells us to.

Gardening too is probably one the best forms of natural therapy there is. Being in your open space, surrounded by plants and flowers that don't answer back, gives you the head space that is often much needed.

Seasonal Vegetable and Fruit Planting

Planting – first you must decide what you would like to grow. You may consider what will realistically get eaten, how much space you have and how much of the plant you can harvest for your efforts. You can start from seed or you can buy young seedling plants from the local garden centre. Below I have listed some suggestions. You may have more space and really enjoy growing your own. If this is the case, research. There are many creative gardeners out there who beautifully incorporate vegetables and fruits into their gardens' landscaping.

Herb – food prepared without herbs is a sad meal. Herbs offer so much flavour and can transform the dullest of dishes into a delectable delight. Not only do herbs offer flavour, they also have medicinal properties too. I have divided the herbs into hardy herbs, that last all year around, and those that prefer warmer temperatures. You can buy herbs from your local garden centre, supermarket and green grocer.

Hardy – these just need to be pruned and the dead stems cut to keep them healthy and plentiful
Rosemary, Bay Leaf, Sage, Thyme, Oregano, Marjoram

Warmer temperatures –
Flat leaf Parsley, Mint, Coriander, Basil, Lemon Verbena

Vegetables – Plant in the summer ready to eat in the late autumn and winter months
Carrots, Beetroot, Swede, Parsnips, Potatoes, Onions, Purple sprouting Broccoli, Kale, Calvo Nero, Spinach, Swiss Chard.

Vegetables – Plant in the spring to be picked in the summer
Sweetcorn, Courgette, Peas, Sugar Snaps, Runner Beans, Mange Tout, French Beans and Lettuce – Rocket, Cos, Baby Gem, Oak leaf.

CHAPTER 19

Relaxed Cooking

Happy cooking creates happy food. What you put into the cooking process aside from the ingredients can really impact on the end result. There is a reason why you always remember certain foods you ate as a child. You associate your mum's cooking with being loved and nurtured. It doesn't matter if you are not the next global MasterChef. Your children love your food because you love them and they can feel it. Children care about food being there for them to eat when they are hungry. Favourite foods can be like a comfort blanket after a shocking day at school. Cooking is an expression of love. Home cooked food permeates the house with lovely smells – it's home, it's comfort, it's great!

My first rule about cooking is don't worry. Recipes are just guidelines – with the exception of desserts, which are a bit more scientific. When the world was created, God didn't hand down a 'cooking manual'. Everything we hold dear to our hearts in the culinary world has been created through trial, error and experimentation. To be a great cook doesn't mean that you need to wear some high hat and chequered trousers. Before there were restaurants, there were mums creating traditional dishes from the local ingredients available to them. They understood their local ingredients and to this day their creations are held in high esteem, inspiring chefs the world over. You can add herbs, spices, seasoning rubs to jazz-up dull dishes, with little effort making a big transformation. Cooking doesn't need to be fancy, just honour the lovely manna of ingredients available to you.

I love cooking. It's what I have done for as long as I can remember.

143

To me cooking is a meditation, I'm completely relaxed and focused on what I am creating. I am not worrying about the things I cannot change. It helps me to find the inner peaceful place. There is something satisfying about creating something that brings joy to others. It is great to introduce children to the ways of the kitchen when they are young. It's family time. You are creating memories, whilst teaching life skills. Put the tunes on, sing into the whisk, be happy and let your kids see you being happy. It's so easy to get caught up in the stresses of life that we often forget to kick back and enjoy the small things. Life is for living and enjoying, even in the 21st century madness.

Eating

Eating should be enjoyed in a balanced way. Saying grace or internalising gratitude to all the different hands that helped put the food on your plate is a great way to start a meal. Why? Because you are honouring your food and respecting those who helped its journey from seed to plate. A lot of food today is eaten unconsciously. We eat too quick, we don't pay attention to what it is. If it's good for us or not, a lot of the time we just eat out of comfort, way past what our body needs. Food becomes fodder when we don't pay it attention. Eat in a peaceful environment, make dinnertime your catch-up time, a time where you can check in with each other.

Eat healthy-sized portions. The correct portion for you should be when you cup your hands together, as that is the size of your stomach. Let's face it if we stretch our stomach the rest of us begins to stretch too – and I am not talking about a yoga stretch, I am talking about the wobble stretch.

After eating, relax for some time, let your food digest effectively and then tidy up. To me there is nothing worse than having to clean up yesterday's dishes when you wake up. Big nights happen and that's great, but on regular days tidy up so that you can walk into your Zen-like kitchen and start your new day the best way you can. If you aren't a fan of washing up, chore it out to the children or invest in a dishwasher.

Daily Cooking Tips

Getting meals ready can sometimes feel like you have just walked onto the set of 'Ready, Steady, Cook', with an audience of famished little people. You can't get the meal prepared quickly enough. On other days, you may feel like you want to do a U-turn straight out of the kitchen, back to the sofa and put your feet up. Some days the kitchen can become your retreat and you fill the house for days with beautiful digestible smells. Being a mum is busy and part of our daily must-do is feeding our children, so how do we do that with minimal stress?

Menu planning – knowing where you are each day with meals stops you from having to make last minute creative decisions. It's an idea to sit down with your children and do the menu plan together, so that they feel included in the choices. Menu planning helps with the shopping lists and ensures that you have the right ingredients in for the meals that you are going to cook. When planning your daily feeds, be sympathetic to the time and your routine.

Dinnertime rituals – divide up the mealtime chores with your children: laying the table, getting the drinks, loading the dishwasher.

Batch cooking – double your recipes and when time is against you, just pull it out the freezer, so you just have to reheat.

Advanced preparation – have salad dressing, curry pastes, etc already in your fridge so that you don't need to do it on a daily basis.

Slow cooker – invest in a slow cooker, also known as crockpot. They cook food, as their name suggests, very slowly. You can prepare a stew and leave it to slowly cook away, whilst you get on with your day.

Nap time/school time – if you have a child still at the napping stage, take advantage of this time or when they are at school, to get some dinner preparations done.

Keep the kids entertained – If your kids are busy and entertaining themselves you can get on and cook. They could be colouring on the kitchen table or doing their homework, playing board games with each other, or watching their TV shows.

Cooking sabbatical – give yourself a permission slip to have a night off. If you want to order in, or buy a ready meal, do so. We all need some time off, so honour how you are feeling.

Have dinner dates with friends and family – organise regular dinner dates with the people that you love and those who are uplifting to be around. You can share the cooking and the cleaning up. It's good for you to have other adult company and for your children to be with other kids. It's also a night out.

Take advantage of the weather – if it's warm and sunny and the nights are light, then go out to the park for a picnic, eat alfresco, have a BBQ. Keep the meals simple, so that it's a way to relax for all of you.

Have the right kitchen utensils and equipment – having sharp, good quality knives, good chopping boards, a food processor, soup blender, good peeler and good-sized mixing bowls will help no end in your food preparations.

Keep a well-stocked larder or dry stores cupboard – start a spice collection. Spices can bring the perfect zing to any meal. Stock up on bottles of Asian seasonings, baking supplies, pulses and grains, noodles and pastas. Having bountiful cupboards gives you mealtime options and quick solutions.

CHAPTER 20

Healthy Eating & Living

Being a mother means many things, but the word you would always equate to a mother is nurture. Feeding your child should always be about nurturing them the best way that you can, so that they may grow up to be healthy and body confident. And if you are feeding your child the best way you can, then you to are going to be giving yourself the best at mealtimes too.

Since the world began turning, our diets have changed dramatically. Presently we live in a world where a lot of food is far removed from its natural state. We are often dependant on high sugar, high fat diets and our eating revolves around cravings, rather than that of our bodies own innate wisdom of what it truly needs.

It's as though a haze fell upon us, creating confusion of what we should eat, with constant media contradiction, dietary fads and seductive advertising playing on our inner most desires. Just for the record, a tub of Belgium chocolate ice cream hasn't bought me a movie star lover, it just made my butt wobble. And, I am yet to meet someone who has been teleported to the Greek islands whilst eating a tub of honeyed Greek yoghurt.

What we should eat and what we want to eat are often two completely different things. In truth, we rarely eat consciously or responsibly for our health. In the developed world, there is a concerning rise in the numbers of cases of obese and morbidly obese children and adult diabetes, heart disease, cancers, allergies and digestive disorders. Bad food is addictive, it's made that way with a cocktail of additives. For example, mono sodium glutamate – MSG – was used during the Second World War on food for Japanese soldiers to stimulate their appetite. It was discovered that putting MSG on bad tasting food suddenly made it palatable. MSG is a chemical that excites our brain and is therefore addictive. Industrialized processed foods are created to stimulate, which makes them addictive and sadly there is very little that is nutritionally good about them. The more addictive something is the more we buy and the more we buy the fatter someone's pockets become.

There is no saying more accurate than 'you are what you eat'. Eating therefore is karma. You react on a physical, emotional and mental level to what you feed yourself. If you eat rubbish, you are going to feel rubbish, but if you eat a varied diet filled with raw and cooked vegetables, fruits, seeds, pulses, low in animal products, omitting confectionery sugars and limited caffeine and alcohol intake, the more energized and vital you will feel. As a lone parent, you need to feel as vital and energized as you possibly can. And if a child is fed foods that are filled with optimum nutrition, it gives them a fantastic start in life, because they will instinctively desire those healthier foods later in their life.

So how to make the change to eat food that is good for you

Eating consciously is eating foods that are good for you. That make your body sing from the inside. Changing habitual eating patterns can seem overwhelming to begin with and it can be a battle but be persistent. Persistence pays off, because you start to feel the benefits from eating a much purer diet. Rather than thinking that you are no longer allowed something, start thinking from a more positive perspective, of the abundant positive new healthy foods and cooking styles that you will be bringing into your and your children's lives.

Have faith that you can make the changes. Write yourself little notes of encouragement, stick pictures of healthy foods and healthy vital people on your kitchen walls for inspiration. Set yourself goals and targets (don't beat yourself up. If at first you don't succeed, try and try again). Detoxify your cupboards, fridge and freezer by getting rid of anything that isn't doing you any favours. Ridding yourself of temptations means they aren't there when the cravings start. Replace them with healthier substitutes. Read labels, as there is often a lot more hidden in foods than we think. Try new recipes. You aren't going to like everything initially, but keep going because after a while you will start to desire these healthier foods and that's your body's innate knowing activating. When your diet becomes purer, you really notice the sluggish or hyper effects that processed foods had on you. Healthy eating is paramount to feeling great.

Emotional Eating

Falling into a pattern of eating for comfort, as a stress relief or to squash down emotions, rather than for need is common. Food is legal, readily available and junk food is highly addictive, with all its pleasure inducing additives. Food then becomes a temporary emotional crutch, to make us feel better. Eating is generally a pleasurable activity. When we feel pleasure, we feel happy. Unfortunately, emotional eating doesn't fix problems and it often makes us feel worse, as we then feel guilty for overeating. Sugar is highly addictive; it is sweet and we often gravitate towards it, to make us feel that life is sweeter than it is.

To overcome emotional eating, you must recognise your emotional eating triggers – stress, boredom, loneliness, sadness etc. Before committing yourself to the tub of ice-cream, the bar of chocolate or the bag of crisps, ask yourself: do you need it?

When you feel the hunger pangs of emotional eating striking, remove yourself from temptation. Divert your attention to something else, or alternatively face your emotions head on, rather than squashing them down with food.

Understand the cause of your emotional eating, keep a food journal with details of your feelings and cravings. Also understand where the habit originated from. As children, many of us where given sweet threats as a reward or to make us feel better, and this becomes woven into our subconscious mind.

If you feel that you are an emotional eater, try Emotional Freedom

Techniques (EFT) or Neuro Linguistic Programming (NLP). These techniques can really help with breaking food dependency patterns and habits.

For sweet dependency, try cinnamon or take the supplement chromium, as this balances blood sugar levels. Doing a mini detox or fast will also help to balance out the cravings and it's a good way to cleanse your body of food dependant substances (sugar, caffeine, salt). Emotional eating is something that can be overcome with some determination.

Creating A Healthy Diet

A healthy diet is a diet filled with foods that are as close to their natural state as possible, the very way Mother Nature intended, with all its life-giving goodness intact. There are many healthy eating approaches out there.

I have dabbled in a fair few approaches of healthy eating, including a raw food diet, vegetarianism, veganism, food combining, alkaline diet, exclusion diets etc. The diet that I have found to work for me and my daughter is mainly vegetarian. If meat or fish is eaten, it is from an ethical and grass fed source. Our general diet is high in vegetables, wholegrains, fruit, pulses, nuts, seeds, herbs, spices and very low in processed food and fried fatty food. My weakness has been chocolate and biscuits, and in times of stress I used to dive bomb into those sugary little treats like you wouldn't believe. Now I have had to find healthier alternatives, for the sake of my general wellbeing.

Balance the Body's Acid Alkaline Conditions

It is a fact that a diet that is high in alkaline balancing foods is best for you. Foods that create acidic conditions in your body aren't. Disease and unbalance can be created in an acid body. As you have probably guessed, highly processed and refined salty, sugary, starchy, fatty foods and drinks, as well as dairy and meat, are the main culprits. Their acidic residue ends up in our bloodstream, changing the body's natural chemistry. This in turn puts a heavier burden on our liver and kidneys, as they then have to break the acidic residue. Symptoms of an acidic body can include depression, mood swings, fatigue and insomnia, skin irritations, dull hair, hair loss, cellulite, sensitive gums, food intolerances, bloating, acne, aching joints etc. Our body is a fine-tuned vehicle and needs to be nourished and looked after for an optimum, joyful life.

Alkaline foods in their cleanest and most natural form are your body's friend. Simply by changing your eating choices you can feel the health benefits. When you choose a more alkaline diet you feel much lighter and energized and how we feel ultimately is how we interact with the world. A great way to start your day is with a lovely warm cup of lemon or apple cider vinegar water, as it balances the stomach acid for the day ahead.

Find Wheat Free Alternatives

Wheat is regularly connected to a sluggish digestion, bloating and allergies. If this sounds familiar, try using alternatives to regular wheat flours – spelt, kamut, quinoa, corn, oats and rye. The supermarkets and health food shops have plenty of alternatives on offer, so that you do not have to eat the overly-refined breads and pastas. Try wheat free breads and sourdough, it's not quite the same but may help you feel better and if you really find it hard to give up the wheat bread, go for artisan bread products or wholemeal seeded organic breads.

Choose Oils Wisely

Choosing the right oils can have a positive effect within every cell in our body. It's not often you hear that, but it is indeed true, if you choose fresh, unrefined and cold pressed oils. Our bodies need essential fatty acids and you can get those from incorporating healthily produced oils into your diet. These include avocado, coconut, flax seed, as well as olive, seed and nut oils.

By replacing all the hydrogenated oils, margarines that contain trans fats, cooked and processed oils that are rife with free radicals, for natural oils you will notice the positive changes to your skin, your hair and nail growth, your digestion and your energy levels will increase. These oils also make excellent non-toxic moisturizers for your skin too.

Reduce Fried Food, Fast Food and Processed Food or Eliminate

This group of foods make us slow, sluggish and tired, and have no positive effect upon our health. I know that it is often convenient, tasty (for all the wrong reasons) and cheap. But by replacing these habits you will see the health rewards, including weight loss, increased energy, clear skin and a capable digestive system. Instead of shallow or deep fried cooking, try baking or steaming as a healthier alternative.

Reduce Dairy

Too much dairy especially processed dairy isn't good for us. Dairy produces mucus in our digestive system making it difficult for effective assimilation and elimination to take place during the digestive process. Switch to organic and if you can and feel like you would like to try cow alternatives there are goat, sheep, buffalo, or even non-dairy alternatives. Raw Diary products are becoming increasingly popular. The first reason being that they come from grass fed organic cattle and secondly, whereby in commercially produced dairy products most of the beneficial enzymes and goodness have been destroyed in the pasteurizing process, raw dairy products still retain these beneficial enzymes.

Find Sugar Alternatives

Regular refined sugar does nothing good for us apart from taste sweet. It causes imbalances, energy crashes, is detrimental to our blood-sugar as well as leeching nutrients from the body. Avoid white sugars, corn syrups, artificial sweeteners containing aspartame (which is toxic) and replace them with coconut palm sugar (the healthiest option) or agave syrup, brown rice syrup, raw honey, fruit syrups and maple syrup. Stevia is a natural plant based sweetener available in liquid or powder.

Begin Sprouting

Sprouting is fantastic and something the children can really get involved with. You can sprout nuts, seeds, beans and grains. It's so easy and involves very little effort for the fantastic sprouts filled with life force. Sprouts are so nutritious and a great accompaniment to salads, sandwiches or they can be used in raw food dishes.

Begin by soaking your chosen seed, nut, bean or grain for between 6-12 hours in clean pure water in a covered glass jar. After they have been soaked, drain them and rinse them again, returning them to the jar, ensuring that no water is left on them. Cover them once again and leave them at a 45-degree angle in daylight. Seeds that have begun to sprout need to be washed and rinsed daily. The sprouts are usually ready to begin harvesting within 2-5 days. Sprouting seeds are available in good health food shops. If you don't like the idea of a jar you can buy a sprouting tray stack. There are other sprouting methods, including the clay method or soil sprouting.

Activating Nuts and Seeds

Nuts and seeds contain many enzymes in them. By soaking them and allowing them to germinate, the enzyme inhibitors are then released, thus bringing the nut to life. Once the nut has soaked for about 12 hours, they are then dehydrated at a temperature of 40 degrees, so the lovely activated enzymes are not destroyed. Activating nuts and seeds makes them more nutrient dense and easier to digest and helps to reduce the acid in them. The natural oils/fats in nuts and seeds are polyunsaturated and can go rancid if not stored properly. Freezing them is a good way to store them effectively.

Drink Fresh Juices, Smoothies and Nut Milk Shakes

Fresh juice and smoothies are one of the quickest ways to get goodness into you. Within minutes of drinking these nutrient-crammed delights, those nutrients are zooming through your bloodstream. To begin with, drinking fresh vegetable juices can seem a bit of an acquired taste, but don't give up, play around with different combos. Children love smoothies, and you can try putting some green leaf vegetables into them. Leafy green vegetables are very alkaline, which of course is a 'thumbs up'. Fruits contain fructose sugar, which although completely natural, is still sugar. So, too much fruit isn't advisable and it would be beneficial to add some greens when you can. If you choose to, you can always add some super food powders into them, to give them even more of health boost.

Eat as Many Whole Foods as You Can

Whole foods are natural foods, including fruits, vegetables, whole grains, pulses, nuts and seeds. Foods filled with fibre, minerals, vitamins, joy and love. Eat a large variety to get the benefit of flavours, textures, tastes, nutrition and interest. Variety, some would say, is the spice of life and with food and diet I would have to agree. So, bin the refined foods and replace them with whole food substitutes.

Eat Fresh Food with Every Meal

It's wonderful if with every meal time you can incorporate some fresh and raw fruit and vegetables into your choices for yourself and your children. Sandwiches can be transformed into vegetable bulging delights, have interesting side salads with your mains, fruit salads, drink powerhouse juices and smoothies, which are bursting with body-love goodness. Snack on freshly-prepared fruit and vegetables with interesting little dips.

Supplements

Supplements are a big subject and if you feel that you are deficient in something, or are experiencing an imbalance, it is advisable to seek professional advice. It's always best to get as many minerals and vitamins as you can from your food. Eating a fresh and varied diet is your body's most natural way to assimilate them, rather than taking a lot of supplements and not changing your diet. I would recommend daily taking a good quality multivitamin, spirulina and an omega booster. During the cold seasons, add immune boosting supplements including Echinacea, Acai, zinc, vitamin A, C and E. As a lone parent stress is often present, simply due to the responsibilities of your daily life. Supplements to help with this are Ashwaganda, St John's Wart, B Complex and magnesium. To help give myself a daily boast of extra nourishment, I take super green powders. These are filled with antioxidants and alkaline, which really help to oxygenate the blood stream.

Super Foods

Super food is the name given to a group of foods that contain huge amounts of nutritional goodness. They are packed with enzymes, minerals, vitamins, anti-oxidants, good fats and oils and they are a clean source protein that have more than one or two unique properties which really nourish the body on many levels – detoxifying, rebalancing and rejuvenating. By adding super foods to your diet, it allows you to get optimum nutrition with less eating. Super foods are detoxifying and help to assist your body repair and rebalance itself from previous eating habits that have led to illness. Examples of super foods are Coconuts, Goji Berries, Maca root, Bee pollen, Spirulina, Aloe Vera, Blue Green Algae, Hempseeds, Wheat grass and Seaweeds.

Probiotics

Probiotic's are essential to our health, they are the good bacteria that are present in our digestive track. The term probiotic means 'good for life'. Begin to see these little organisms as your gut's protective little friends, defending against disease and actively working to promote health in you. A bad diet and excessive use of antibiotics and other medicines depletes your body probiotics. You can find probiotics in health food shops in powder or capsule form, or alternatively you can eat and drink cultured and fermented foods. These include natural sugar free yogurt, sauerkraut, raw apple cider vinegar, Kampuchea tea, pickles and kefir.

Learn and Experiment with Healthy Foods

To begin your new journey, try introducing the new ingredients gradually. Explain to your children the reason for the changes and the benefits of eating a healthier diet – use top athletes, pop icons etc as role models as those who eat healthy diets. Let them help you prepare some of the new dishes, so that they feel completely involved in the process. They can help with juicing, making smoothies and with vegetable preparation (they are learning great skills too). To begin with you may not like some of the new choices but play around with new recipes. Don't give up, keep persisting because in time you will be knocking up some real gems of mealtime taste sensations. There are so many wonderful cooks out there to take inspiration from.

Drinks

Ditch the fizz, the caffeine, the alcohol and the overly concentrated sweetened fruit juices. If that sounds super extreme, then cut down, just limit your intake. Water is what your bodies and minds are crying out for. Hydration only happens with pure fresh water. Our bodies need to stay hydrated to function efficiently.

Physical Exercise

Exercise is key to vitality. I know as a single parent you are busy, non-stop and knackered. The thought of finding another 20 minutes a day to fit in a bit of exercise is a bit like being asked to find the gold at the end of the rainbow. As single mums, we have already a vast multi-tasking foundation, so why not multi-task some exercise into your day? Walk the kids to school, run to the shops, choose the stairs, play active games with your kids outside or watch (and take part in) exercise DVDs.

If you can take an exercise class of your choice one evening a week, that would be a great way to reclaim a bit of you. The time you invest in exercise, you get back in energy. It's stress-busting, body toning and it gives you a spring in your step. Attending new classes gives you the opportunity to meet new people. I would always find an excuse not to exercise – the excuses kept me on the sofa chomping on chocolate and excuses aren't your friend, however convincing they may sound. Exercise is the key!

I know that the above may look and feel quite daunting, but don't worry. Make gradual changes when you feel ready. Do make the changes one day though, because you and your children will reap the benefits. Just add a few more positive alternatives to your lifestyle and diet, and let the old slip away gracefully, rather than immediately excluding things – which may cause some attachment issues to arise, and creating resistance to the new changes. Gradual improvement is the safest way to approach this and you'll see the benefits emerge gradually too.

On A Positive Note

I started this book with my woeful tale of my forced entry into 'singleparentdom'. I was massively resistant to being a single mother. I felt a failure, out of my depth, overwhelmed with responsibility. Not only had my husband screwed me over, so had life itself. I was not in my finest headspace, but I was determined to make it work.

Over time, I began to emerge from a cloudy cocoon of fear into a new life and a new reality. And that's the thing with life – it really is what you make it. We are the creators of our lives, by the various choices we make. Some work out, some choices are our teachers (my marriage certainly has taught me more about myself than any other experience has) and some don't work out, because it simply wasn't right for us.

In the seven years that I have been parenting solo, I have learned to trust life and have faith that stuff does work out – not always the way I want it to, but sometimes what I want is surpassed with what turns up. My focus to begin with was to heal myself, tidy up the path of financial destruction that my ex-husband had left me with and of course, my number one priority was to bring up a healthy, happy, grounded little girl.

I haven't met a new forever man, but if I listen in the distance I can hear the church bells ringing and I am trotting down the aisle to commit to Mr Dazzler. Each relationship and friendship has helped me to learn to trust again. I really closed down emotionally to men and to the idea of a relationship. I had been so hurt, my trust in my own judgement was shot and the thought of opening myself up to a great love just made me feel so vulnerable. Subconsciously I would pick men who were kind and gentle, but also men who had slight commitment issues and who were looking mainly for freedom to continue their nomadic life or friendship.

So, what are the joys of becoming a single parent? Well there are many, it's not always obvious, especially when you have very young children who demand so much of your time. It's super-easy to get lost in the humdrum of life and feeling exhausted. But at the end of the day, you have your own little people, your own creation and wow, so many people would love that. When young ones become more independent, you can slowly recreate your life. Asking for help is humbling. Most people are thrilled to help you out from time to time, although no one likes their kindness to be taken advantage of.

Relationships are hard work. I often observe my married friends and am sometimes witness to moments of tenseness. At those times, I think: "Whoo hoo, I am single, no drama, no rules". I have personal freedom and I can make my own choices, without having to justify them to anyone. Although there are many times that I wish I could sit on the sofa and just have someone who loves me unconditionally. But then I remember that I have my beautiful daughter. And that is one of the most amazing bonuses of being parent in any guise – having that love, that bond and that time with a little innocent person, before they get big and independent. Just stepping off the conveyor belt of chores and spending time with them, listening to their little babbles of thoughts and feelings, puts life and love into perspective. It's a gift! The relationship between you and your children is the best. Me and my girl are buddies and as she gets older, we certainly have more of a laugh together. She can even sometimes (if she is willing and slightly bribed) help around the house. It's a joy to watch her grow and interact with the world and develop her character. I feel blessed to be able to be her mother.

It's not easy for her, as she hasn't seen her dad in years. He has dropped off our radar and we have no idea where he is, we receive the odd phone calls. I am sure one day there will come a time where my daughter is ready to see him. Part of my job is to make her strong, so that she can deal with coming face-to-face with the man she is a part of, yet who has chosen not to show much interest in her life. That takes strength for a child. Rejection is something that can hurt us, in all our challenges and future relationships. For her it is making her stronger, learning to have faith and love for herself. I constantly tell her that her dad couldn't handle the responsibilities that come with being a father, although that doesn't mean that he doesn't love her, he just can't step up to the "father" plateau, and really he is hurting because of that. There is no point at harbouring anger towards him forgiveness and compassion are the key to set us all free.

When my daughter was eight, we had officially outgrown our flat. My body couldn't really cope with sleeping on the sofa any longer. I had a good job and I was surrounded by people whom I adored and valued, and they me, but the job was changing in a way that I didn't want to. My options were limited. A flat with an extra room would cost significantly more cash that I would be able to get my hands on with outselling off my body parts, so I made the plan to jump the Suburban ship and head to the country—good schools, different work opportunities and new possibilities. It was a gamble. We found a little house, which was somewhere that had the potential to be created into a new home. I took on the lease of a local seasonal café. We bought a puppy and our life was suddenly very different. We met new people, who have become great and fabulous friends. The support for my daughter that I was most concerned about manifested almost instantly. Before I knew it, I was running my own business and acting as a consultant chef to a super food company. It was a gamble and life was hectic in the height of the café's peak season. In fact, it was a baptism of fire and it wasn't plain sailing, but it was change and I had found the strength and trust within myself to make it happen, which was huge because for a long time I was stuck in a rut.

I have experienced a huge amount of independence in the last couple of years. On many levels, it's been quite hard to balance the whole 'doing it solo' vibe, finding the belief in oneself that you can do it all, that you can keep rising above the obstacles that life puts in your way. When the buck starts, and stops with you, you connect to an inner strength within yourself and the tendency towards needing others dissipates. You find wholeness in yourself, because you have been doing it for yourself. With wholeness and a willingness to try and take life into your own hands, comes freedom. The freedom of making the choices in your life, for yourself and your children, until a time when they reach their maturity and they can choose their own experiences and lessons. Freedom is a gift and for many years of being a single parent I felt burdened by the responsibility and trapped by being alone. But I play life by my own rules and that's freedom.

It's not to say that I love being alone, but I have learnt to see the positives, especially during the times I spend with bickering couples. I feel some sort of relief. During these years of being alone, I have got to know myself, so that when I do meet someone new I am not going to morph into him and lose myself like I did in my marriage. You have been given a golden card to create a new life, a new fresh sparkly beginning. I know it doesn't feel that way, when all your hopes and dreams about your married life come crumbling down around you. When that golden ring slips off the finger and you know it's over. The divorce papers are signed and it's over.

In a new beginning, it feels that life allows your kids themselves to input into their own hopes and dreams for their own future, so you can all grow together. The communication with your children is great and its fun having common goals—like maybe a place to visit, a holiday, travel. You can all work towards creating that, saving a bit of money and getting excited for your family trip. Saving up money for happy days, happy holidays and setting stuff up to look forward to. Being happy just because you are you, accepting yourself and knowing that you can be happy and whole will attract another happy and whole person to you. A relationship is about complementing and enhancing each other, rather than a love that is based on need.

As human beings, we all need to show each other support and kindness. If there was more selflessness and support in the world, then there would be so much more unity. Wow imagine that! Support is vital when you are a solo parent and in finding support, you don't feel like an island – you feel like a continent. I have friends whose husbands often work away from home, so even if they are not single mums, they still have alone time due to their hubbies' work commitments. So, we get together for communal suppers, days out and fun times. We are there to support one another in friendship, like a sisterhood. We can all air our woes, concerns and joys with each other and get different perspectives. Friends help you to reach your potential, or help you find a better direction—they are not going to let you go out with Mr Wrong, they can see if you are struggling and offer help and a fresh perspective.

Support can come from many places, not just friends and family, but from organisations that you may be involved with. And if you aren't involved in anything then get involved in things that spark your interest. Spiritual/religious-based organisations often have people within their walls whom are more heart centred and wanting to be charitable, kind and supportive. Love comes from many directions – just because you may be single, doesn't mean that you are not loved.

Self-love, self-nurture and being positive encourages living positively. Take time out of being single to take care of yourself, so that you have more love and energy to share with the world. Retain your self-respect and don't ever think that you are worth anything less than respect. Ultimately, it's your life, your responsibility – make it matter, make it golden. Find your happiness and discover the bliss that lies within you and your potential. Above all, give yourself the love that you would desire from a new mate—make yourself the love of your life so you can live life to its fullest.

Contacts That May Help

Gingerbread (single parent support)
Tel- 0808 802 0925
https://gingerbread.org.uk

Citizens Advice
Tel- 03444 111444
https://www.citizenadvice.org.uk

Get a divorce-GOV.UK
http://www.gov.uk.divorce

Child Tax Credits –GOV.UK
https://www.gov.uk >overview

Child Tax Credit- Money Advice Service
https://www.moneyadviceservice.org.uk

Support Line (for addictions)
Tel- 01708765200
www.supportline.org.uk
The website has all the phone number on for all times of addictions

Depression UK
Tel- 02074030888
www.depressionuk.org

The Bereavement Trust
Tel- 0800435455
bereavement-trust.org.uk

Indigo Essences
www.indigoessences.com

Bailey Flower Essences
baileyessences.com

Our Family Wizard
Useful website for help with co parenting
www.ourfamilywizard.co.uk

Support for separated dads
www.separateddads.co.uk

OnlyDads.org
Advise and Support for Single Dads
www.onlydads.org

About the Author

Trudy's first-hand experiences as a single mother bringing up a daughter taught her a lot about herself, her family and network of friends. The learning process she went through led her to write this book, which looks at how to thrive and survive while bringing up children as a single parent. Trudy has encountered and overcome numerous challenges and her experiences are recounted in this fascinating, enlightening read.

Lightning Source UK Ltd.
Milton Keynes UK
UKOW01f1308241017
311560UK00006B/654/P